TREE OF LOVE

THE
YELLOW·JAR
TWO·TALES·FROM·JAPANESE·TRADITION
VOLUME I
PATRICK·ATANGAN
WITH·AN·INTRODUCTION·BY
P·CRAIG·RUSSELL

SILK TAPESTRY
AND OTHER CHINESE FOLKTALES
SONGS OF OUR ANCESTORS
PATRICK ATANGAN

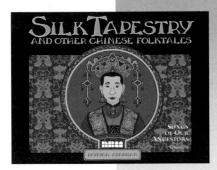

TREE OF LOVE

SONGS OF OUR ANCESTORS
VOLUME III

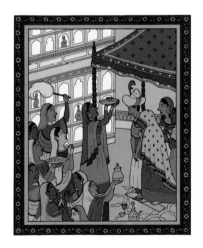

PATRICK ATANGAN

NANTIER · BEALL · MINOUSTCHINE
Publishing inc.
new york

Library of Congress Cataloging-in-Publication Data

Atangan, Patrick.
    The tree of love / Patrick Atangan.
        p. cm. -- (Songs of our ancestors ; v. 3)
    ISBN 1-56163-438-7 (pbk. : alk. paper)
    1. Graphic novels. I. Title. II. Series.

PN6727.A87T74 2005
741.5'973--dc22

                                                    2005050523

                            ISBN-10: 1-56163-438-7
                          ISBN-13: 978-1-56163-438-5
                            © 2005 Patrick Atangan
                                Printed in China

                            5   4   3   2   1

ONCE THERE WAS A YOUNG PRINCE, WHO RULED WITH A GENTLY BENEVOLENCE.

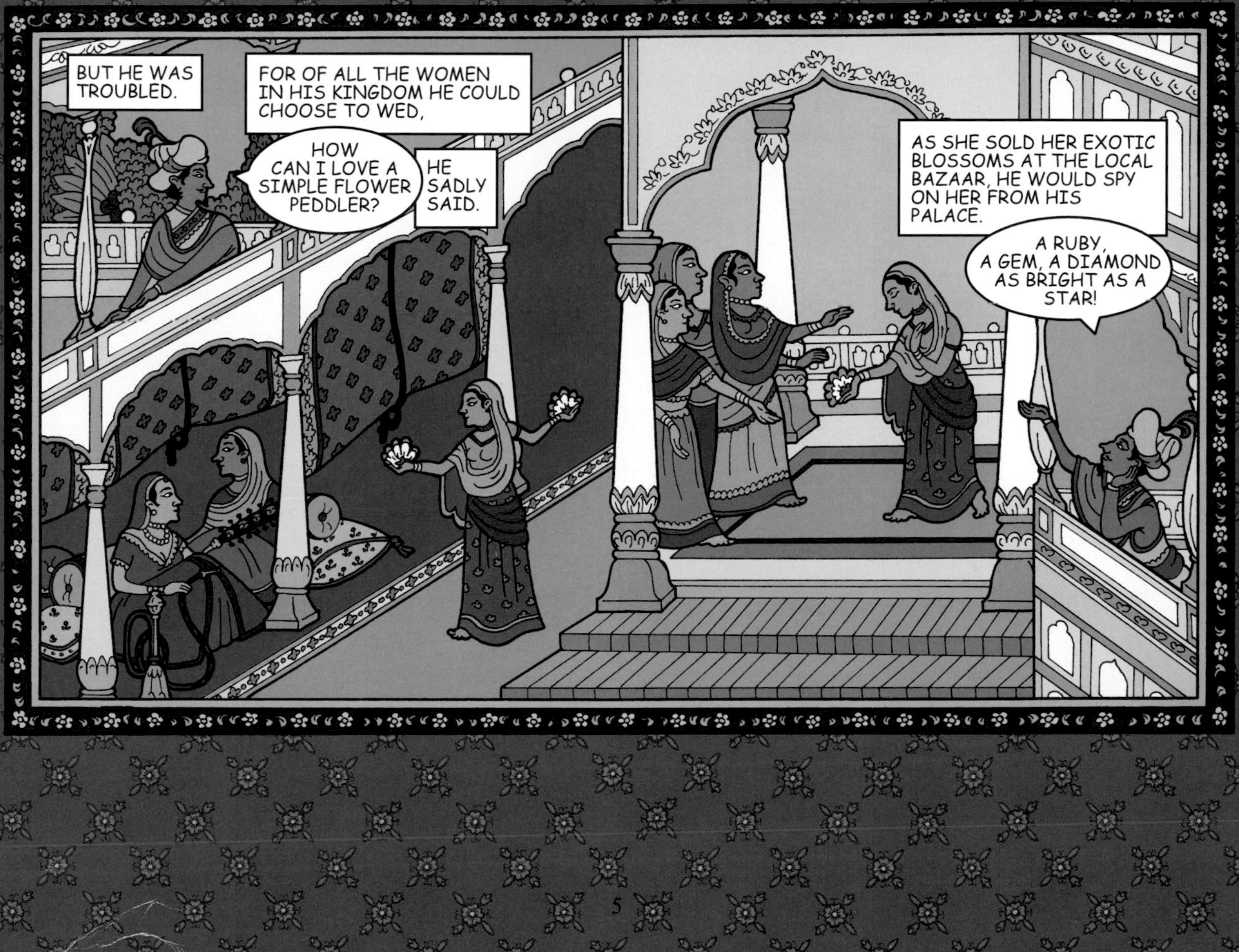
BUT HE WAS TROUBLED.
FOR OF ALL THE WOMEN IN HIS KINGDOM HE COULD CHOOSE TO WED,
HOW CAN I LOVE A SIMPLE FLOWER PEDDLER?
HE SADLY SAID.
AS SHE SOLD HER EXOTIC BLOSSOMS AT THE LOCAL BAZAAR, HE WOULD SPY ON HER FROM HIS PALACE.
A RUBY, A GEM, A DIAMOND AS BRIGHT AS A STAR!

ONE DAY HIS MOTHER CAME TO HIM.

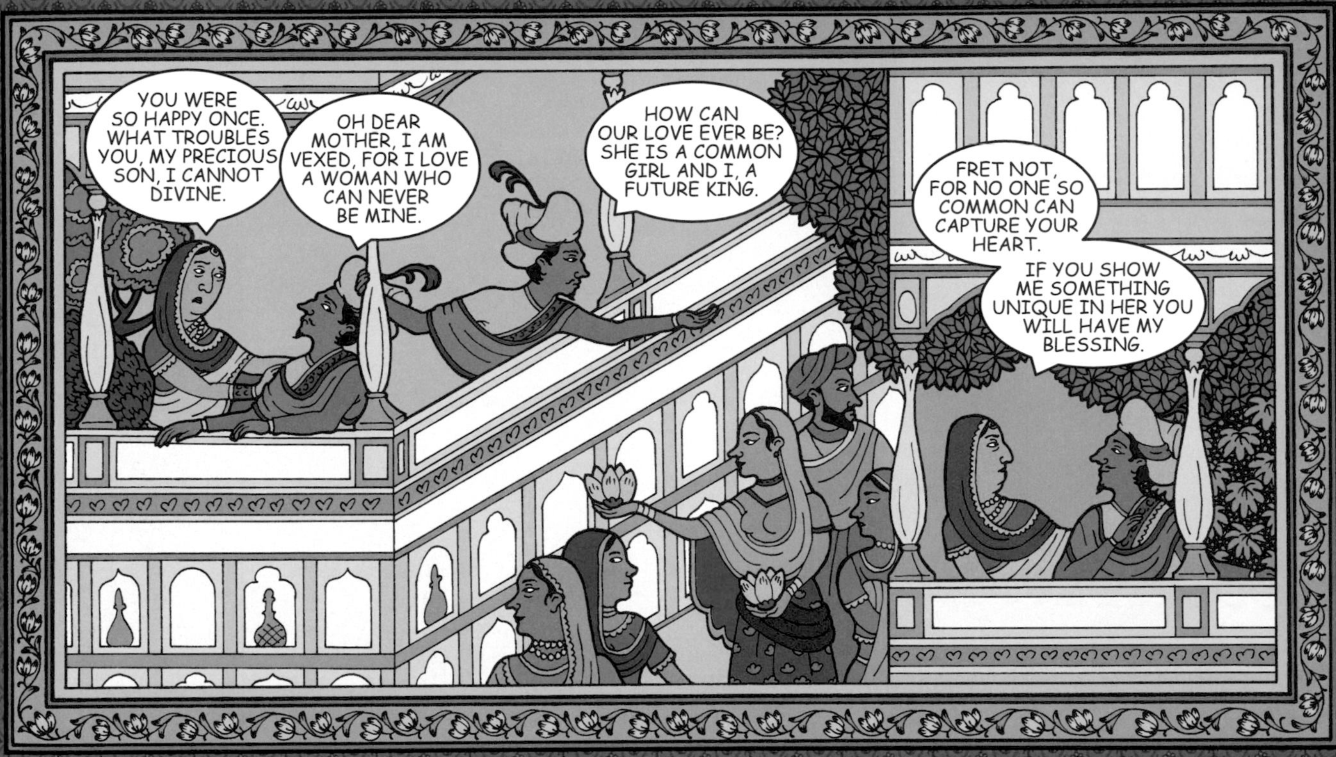

YOU WERE SO HAPPY ONCE. WHAT TROUBLES YOU, MY PRECIOUS SON, I CANNOT DIVINE.
OH DEAR MOTHER, I AM VEXED, FOR I LOVE A WOMAN WHO CAN NEVER BE MINE.
HOW CAN OUR LOVE EVER BE? SHE IS A COMMON GIRL AND I, A FUTURE KING.
FRET NOT, FOR NO ONE SO COMMON CAN CAPTURE YOUR HEART.
IF YOU SHOW ME SOMETHING UNIQUE IN HER YOU WILL HAVE MY BLESSING.

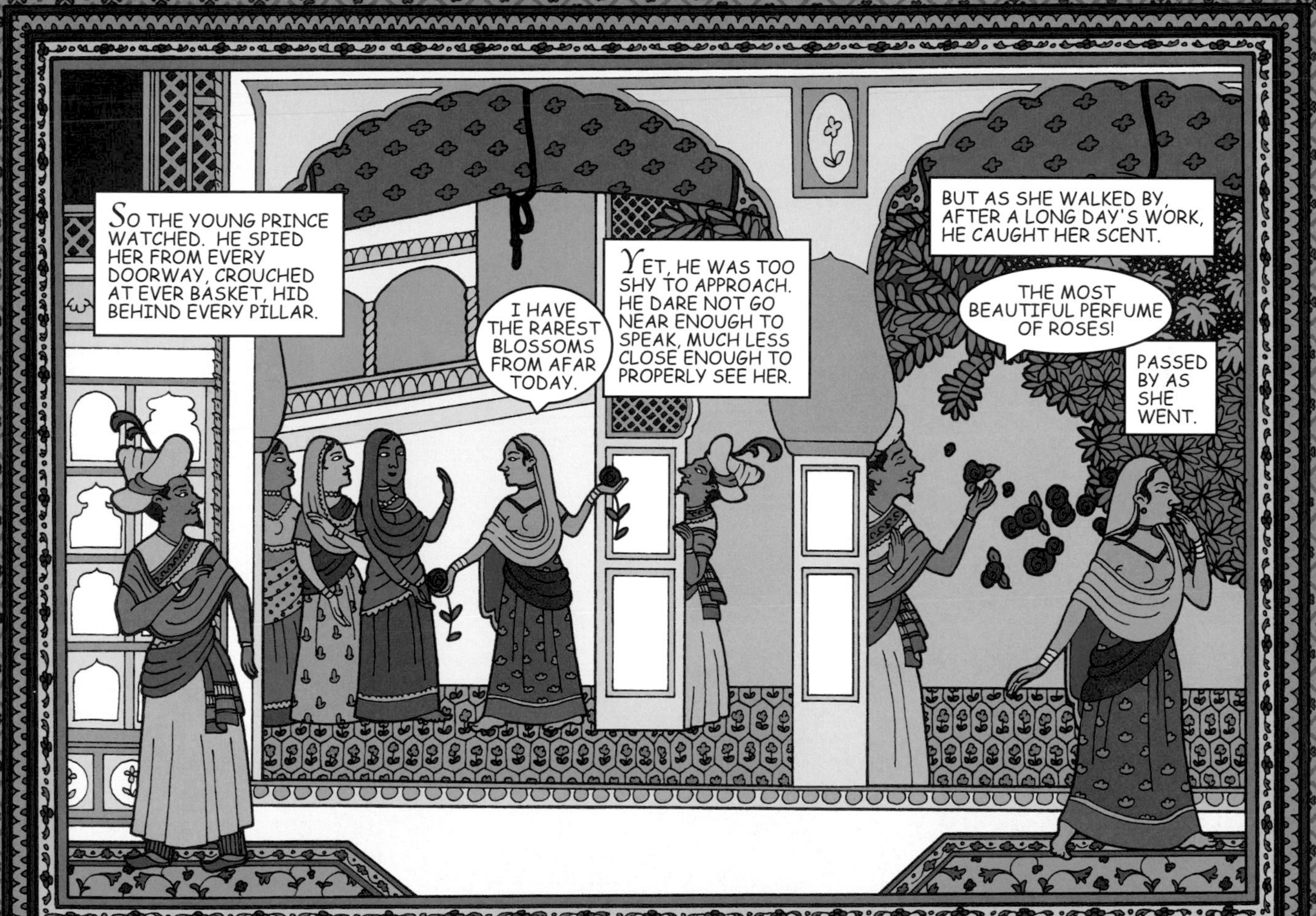
SO THE YOUNG PRINCE WATCHED. HE SPIED HER FROM EVERY DOORWAY, CROUCHED AT EVER BASKET, HID BEHIND EVERY PILLAR.
I HAVE THE RAREST BLOSSOMS FROM AFAR TODAY.
YET, HE WAS TOO SHY TO APPROACH. HE DARE NOT GO NEAR ENOUGH TO SPEAK, MUCH LESS CLOSE ENOUGH TO PROPERLY SEE HER.
BUT AS SHE WALKED BY, AFTER A LONG DAY'S WORK, HE CAUGHT HER SCENT.
THE MOST BEAUTIFUL PERFUME OF ROSES!
PASSED BY AS SHE WENT.

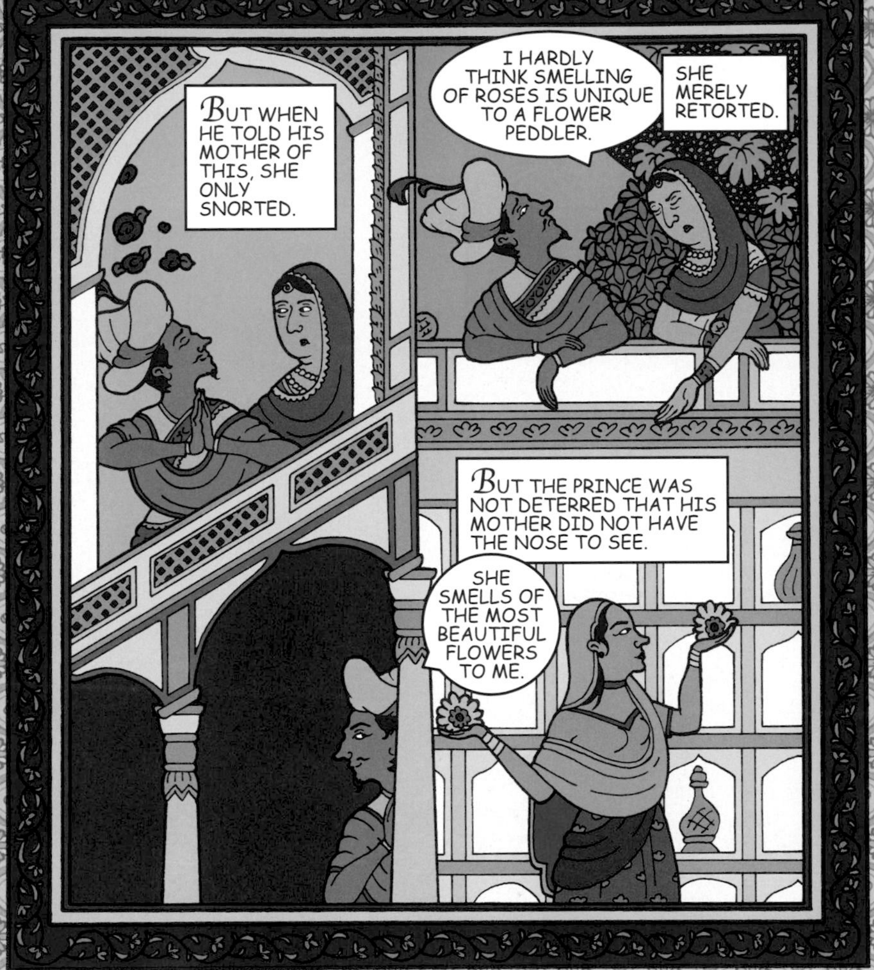
BUT WHEN HE TOLD HIS MOTHER OF THIS, SHE ONLY SNORTED.
I HARDLY THINK SMELLING OF ROSES IS UNIQUE TO A FLOWER PEDDLER.
SHE MERELY RETORTED.
BUT THE PRINCE WAS NOT DETERRED THAT HIS MOTHER DID NOT HAVE THE NOSE TO SEE.
SHE SMELLS OF THE MOST BEAUTIFUL FLOWERS TO ME.

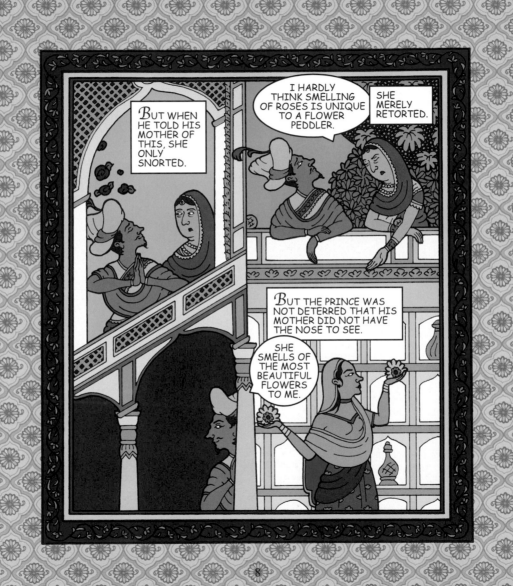

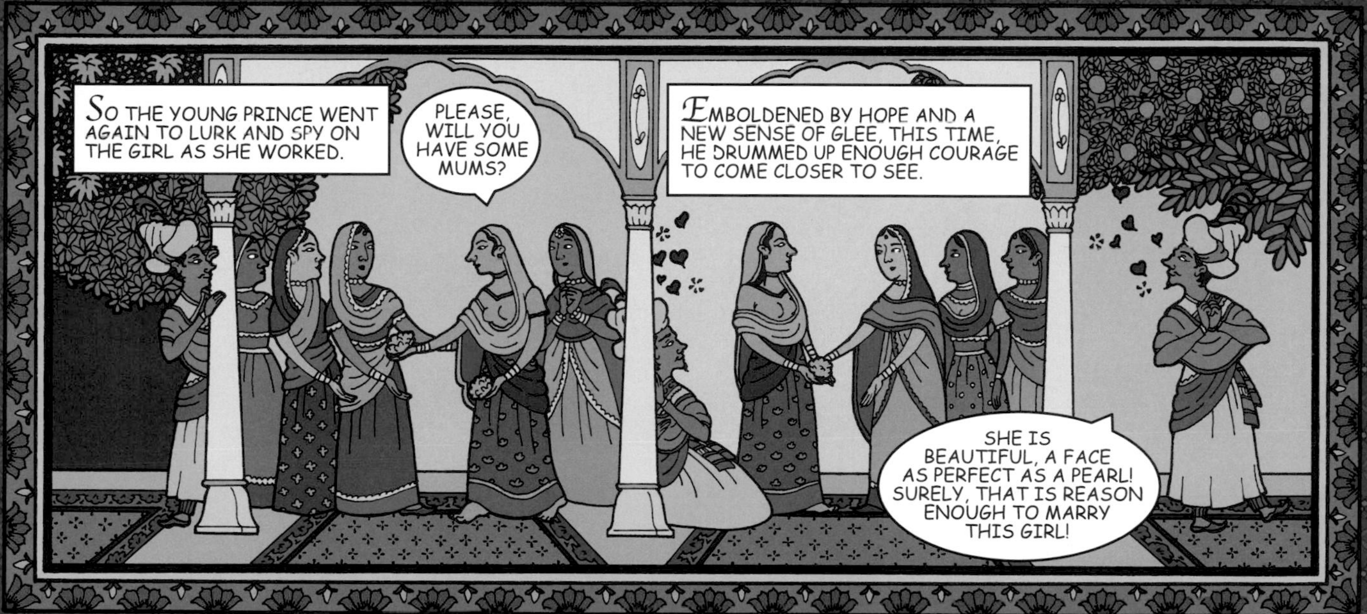
SO THE YOUNG PRINCE WENT AGAIN TO LURK AND SPY ON THE GIRL AS SHE WORKED.
PLEASE, WILL YOU HAVE SOME MUMS?
EMBOLDENED BY HOPE AND A NEW SENSE OF GLEE, THIS TIME, HE DRUMMED UP ENOUGH COURAGE TO COME CLOSER TO SEE.
SHE IS BEAUTIFUL, A FACE AS PERFECT AS A PEARL! SURELY, THAT IS REASON ENOUGH TO MARRY THIS GIRL!

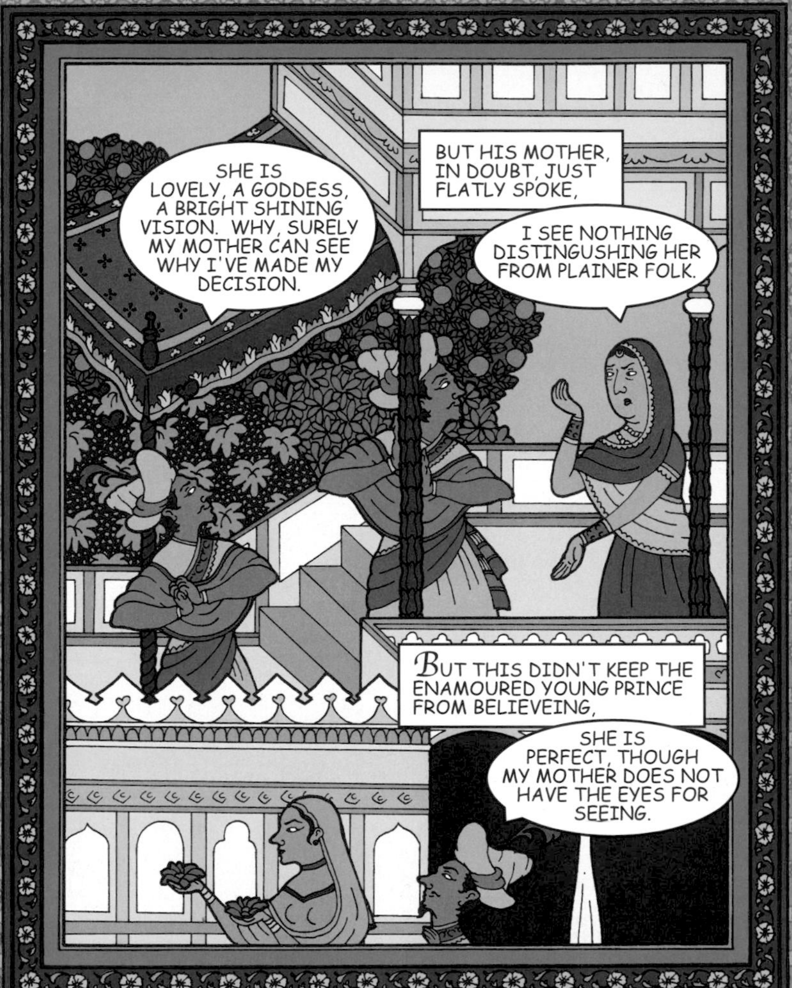

SHE IS LOVELY, A GODDESS, A BRIGHT SHINING VISION. WHY, SURELY MY MOTHER CAN SEE WHY I'VE MADE MY DECISION.
BUT HIS MOTHER, IN DOUBT, JUST FLATLY SPOKE,
I SEE NOTHING DISTINGUSHING HER FROM PLAINER FOLK.
BUT THIS DIDN'T KEEP THE ENAMOURED YOUNG PRINCE FROM BELIEVEING,
SHE IS PERFECT, THOUGH MY MOTHER DOES NOT HAVE THE EYES FOR SEEING.

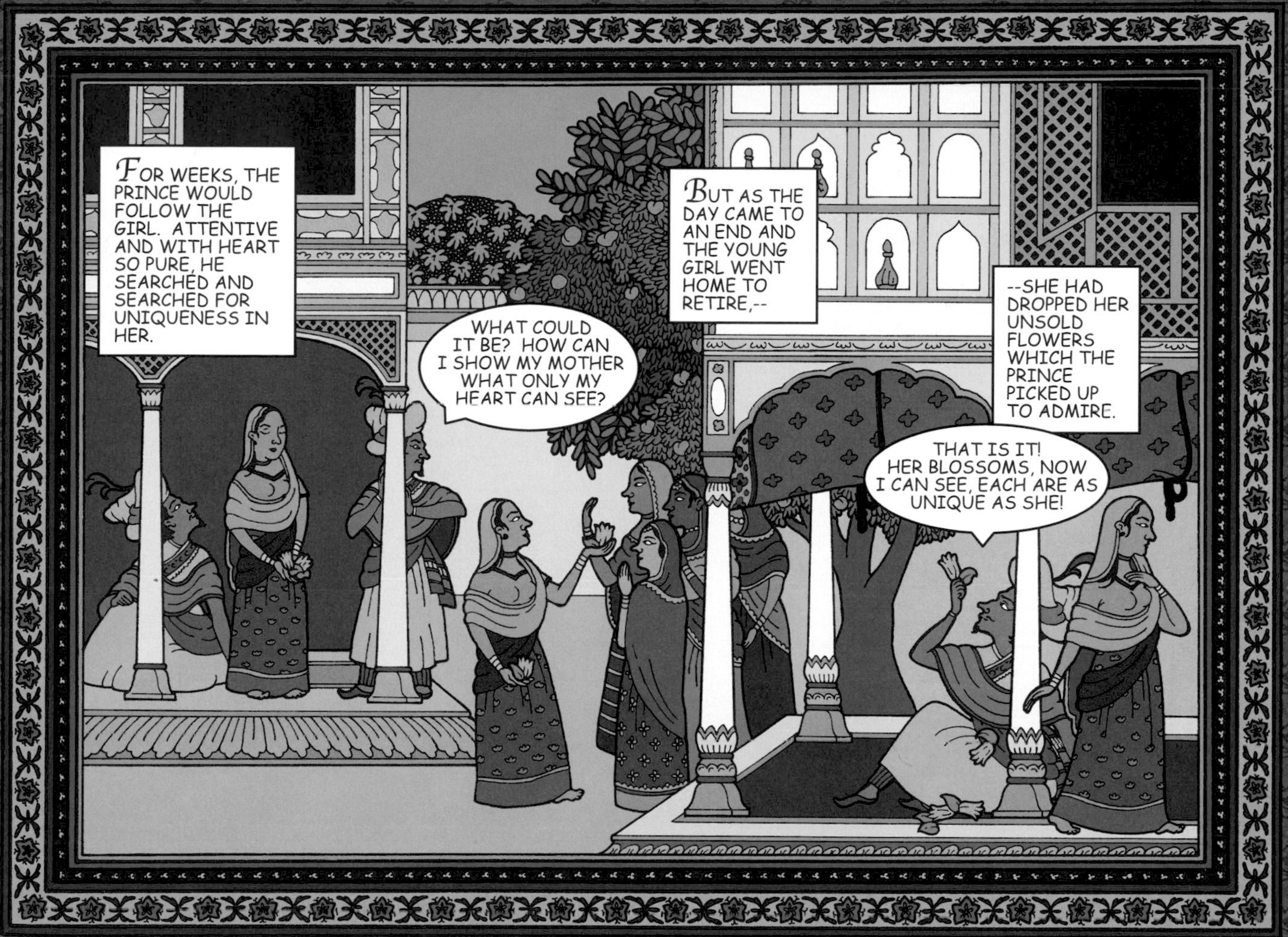
FOR WEEKS, THE PRINCE WOULD FOLLOW THE GIRL. ATTENTIVE AND WITH HEART SO PURE, HE SEARCHED AND SEARCHED FOR UNIQUENESS IN HER.
WHAT COULD IT BE? HOW CAN I SHOW MY MOTHER WHAT ONLY MY HEART CAN SEE?
BUT AS THE DAY CAME TO AN END AND THE YOUNG GIRL WENT HOME TO RETIRE,--
--SHE HAD DROPPED HER UNSOLD FLOWERS WHICH THE PRINCE PICKED UP TO ADMIRE.
THAT IS IT! HER BLOSSOMS, NOW I CAN SEE, EACH ARE AS UNIQUE AS SHE!

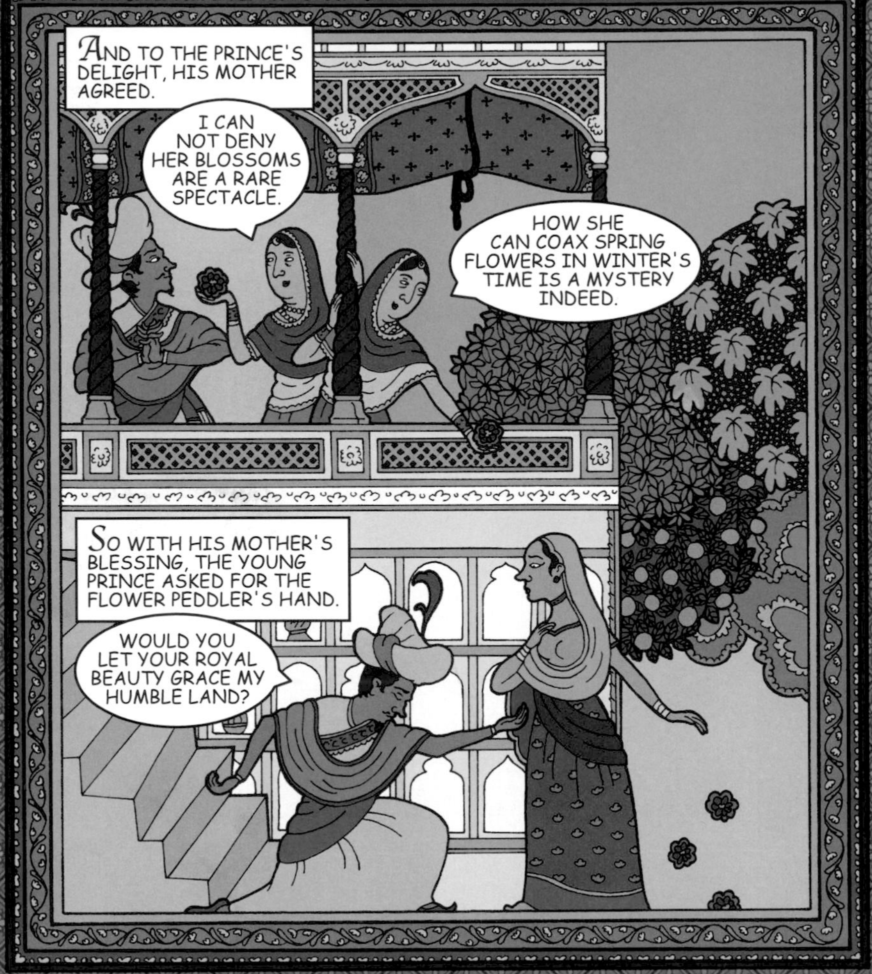
AND TO THE PRINCE'S DELIGHT, HIS MOTHER AGREED.
I CAN NOT DENY HER BLOSSOMS ARE A RARE SPECTACLE.
HOW SHE CAN COAX SPRING FLOWERS IN WINTER'S TIME IS A MYSTERY INDEED.
SO WITH HIS MOTHER'S BLESSING, THE YOUNG PRINCE ASKED FOR THE FLOWER PEDDLER'S HAND.
WOULD YOU LET YOUR ROYAL BEAUTY GRACE MY HUMBLE LAND?

BUT THE FAIR FLOWER PEDDLER ONLY REPLIED,

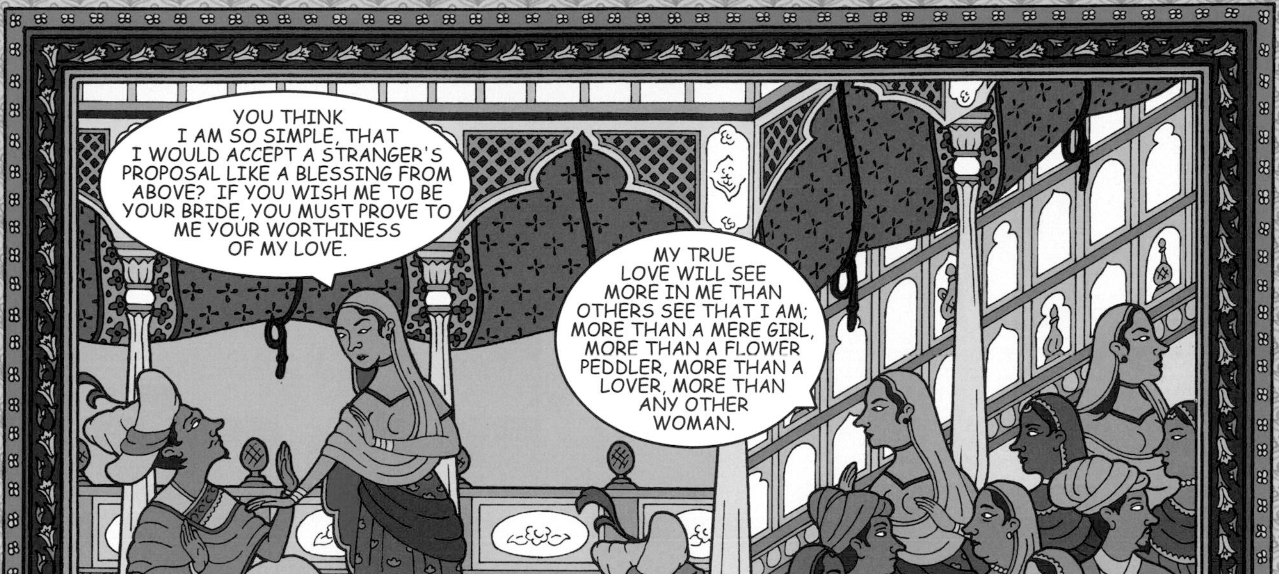
YOU THINK I AM SO SIMPLE, THAT I WOULD ACCEPT A STRANGER'S PROPOSAL LIKE A BLESSING FROM ABOVE? IF YOU WISH ME TO BE YOUR BRIDE, YOU MUST PROVE TO ME YOUR WORTHINESS OF MY LOVE.
MY TRUE LOVE WILL SEE MORE IN ME THAN OTHERS SEE THAT I AM; MORE THAN A MERE GIRL, MORE THAN A FLOWER PEDDLER, MORE THAN A LOVER, MORE THAN ANY OTHER WOMAN.
WITH THE PRINCE IN TEARS HE WEPT, SHE LEFT HIM HOLDING A HANDFUL OF VIOLETS.

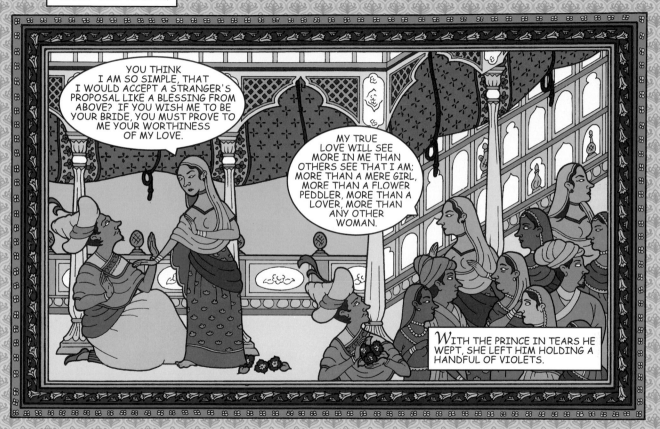

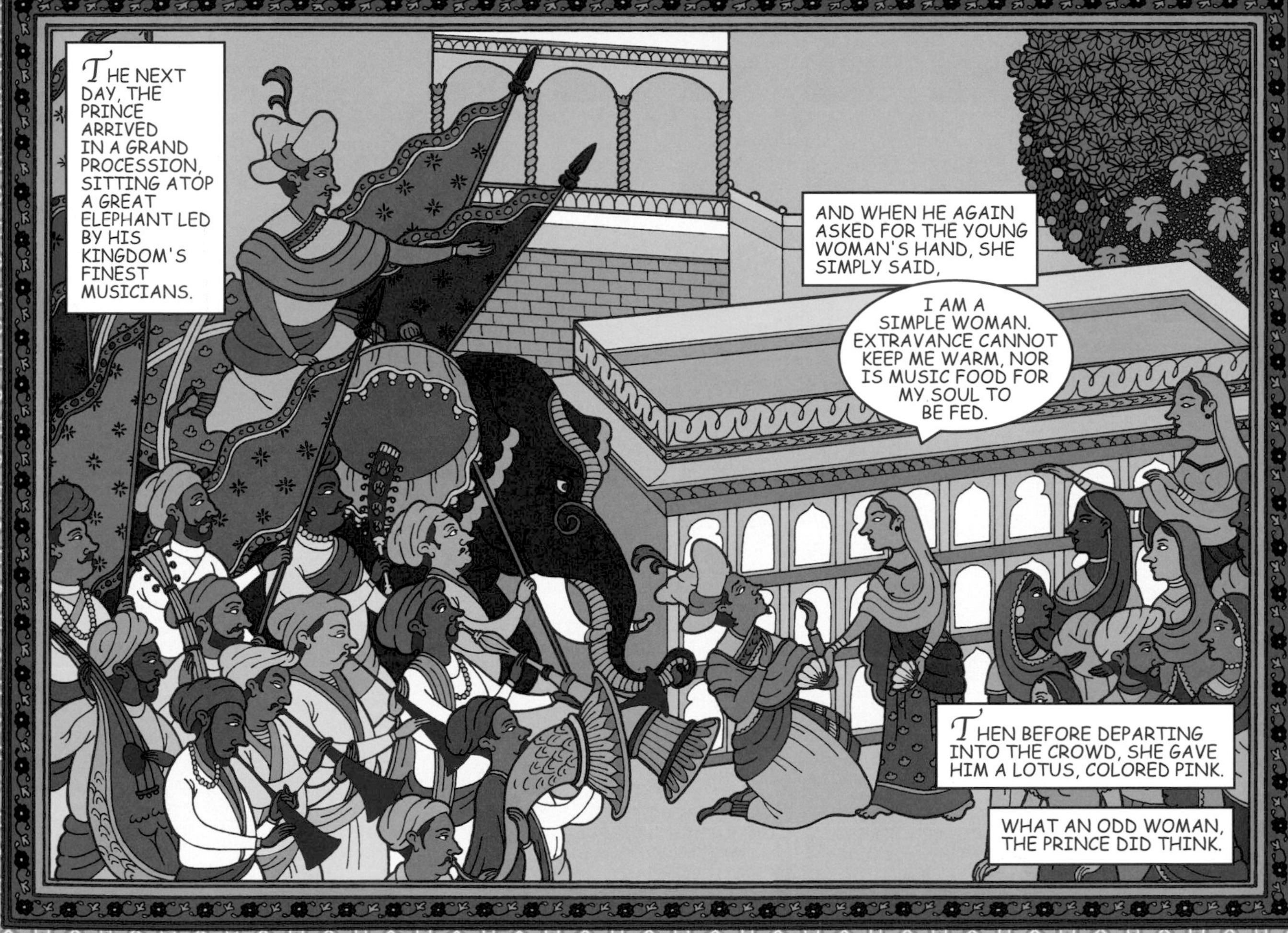
THE NEXT DAY, THE PRINCE ARRIVED IN A GRAND PROCESSION, SITTING ATOP A GREAT ELEPHANT LED BY HIS KINGDOM'S FINEST MUSICIANS.
AND WHEN HE AGAIN ASKED FOR THE YOUNG WOMAN'S HAND, SHE SIMPLY SAID,
I AM A SIMPLE WOMAN. EXTRAVANCE CANNOT KEEP ME WARM, NOR IS MUSIC FOOD FOR MY SOUL TO BE FED.
THEN BEFORE DEPARTING INTO THE CROWD, SHE GAVE HIM A LOTUS, COLORED PINK.
WHAT AN ODD WOMAN, THE PRINCE DID THINK.

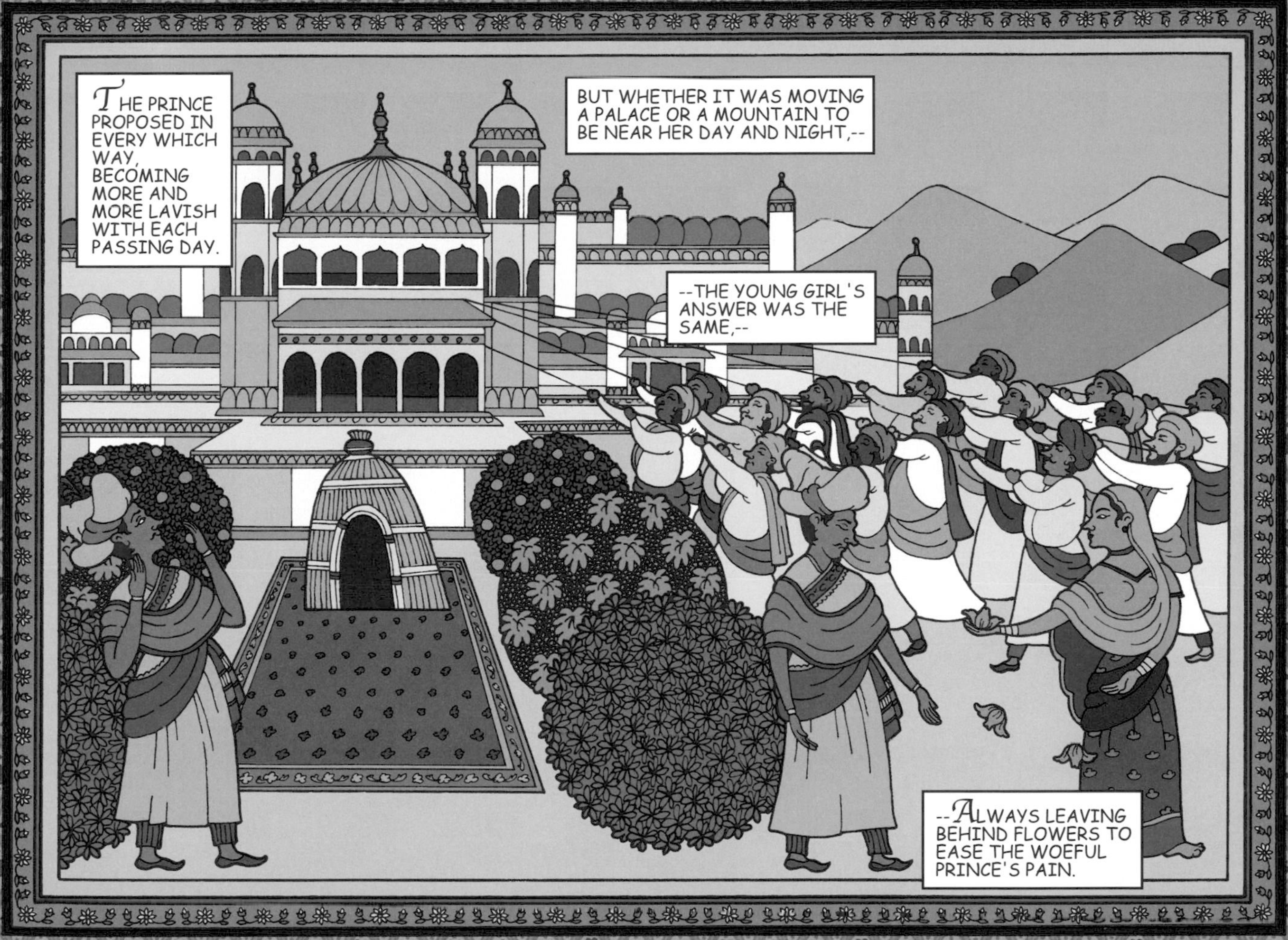
THE PRINCE PROPOSED IN EVERY WHICH WAY, BECOMING MORE AND MORE LAVISH WITH EACH PASSING DAY.
BUT WHETHER IT WAS MOVING A PALACE OR A MOUNTAIN TO BE NEAR HER DAY AND NIGHT,--
--THE YOUNG GIRL'S ANSWER WAS THE SAME,--
--ALWAYS LEAVING BEHIND FLOWERS TO EASE THE WOEFUL PRINCE'S PAIN.

His heartful attempts soon brought a god's favor,--

--who kept monsoon clouds from foaming out the moon so the prince's proposal may be delivered.

But once again, she turned him away,--

I SEEK A LOVE FAR MORE MOVING THAN THESE STARS DRAPED IN NIGHT.

--then gave him a handful of mums that seemed to glow in the quartermoon light.

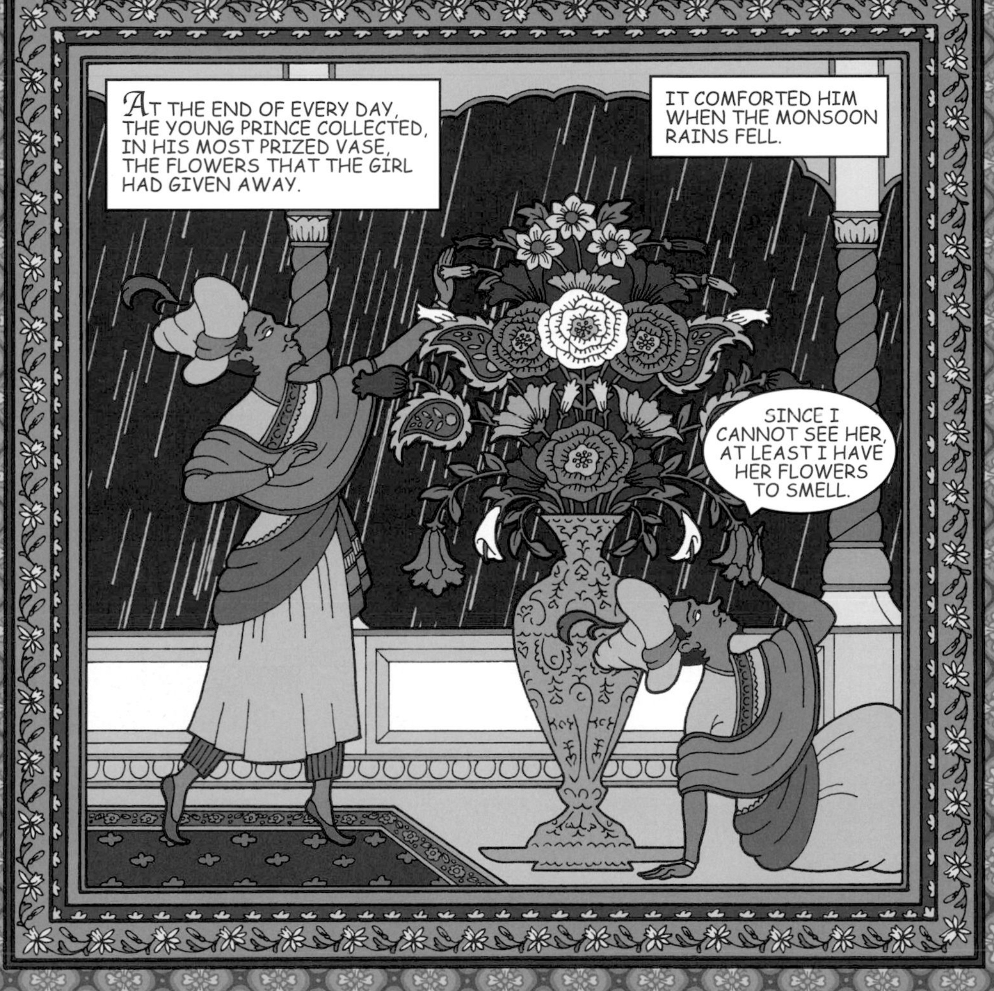
AT THE END OF EVERY DAY, THE YOUNG PRINCE COLLECTED, IN HIS MOST PRIZED VASE, THE FLOWERS THAT THE GIRL HAD GIVEN AWAY.
IT COMFORTED HIM WHEN THE MONSOON RAINS FELL.
SINCE I CANNOT SEE HER, AT LEAST I HAVE HER FLOWERS TO SMELL.

THE RAINS LASTED FOR WEEKS.
IT SEEMED UNENDING.

BUT EVEN THE TIME AWAY FROM HIS LOVE WOULD NOT APPEASE HIS YEARNING.
HE WAS LEFT TO WONDER,
HOW CAN I SHOW HER I TRULY LOVE HER?
SO HE WENT TO WORK, WEAVING A GREAT RUG, SEWING THE VERY FLOWERS SHE GAVE HIM INTO IT AS A SYMBOL OF HIS LOVE.
AT LAST, MY RUG IS FINALLY DONE. NOW, MY FAIR BEAUTY'S LOVE CAN BE WON.

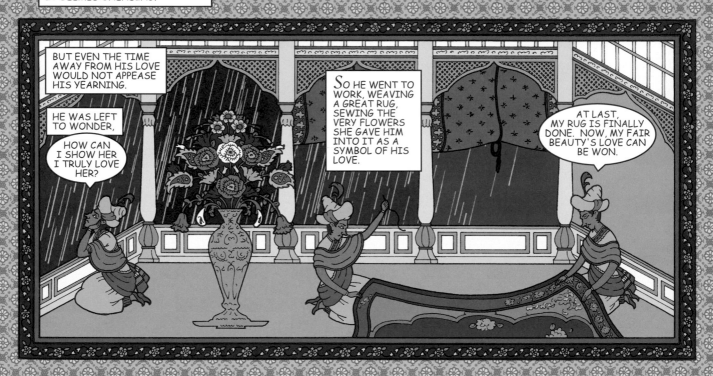

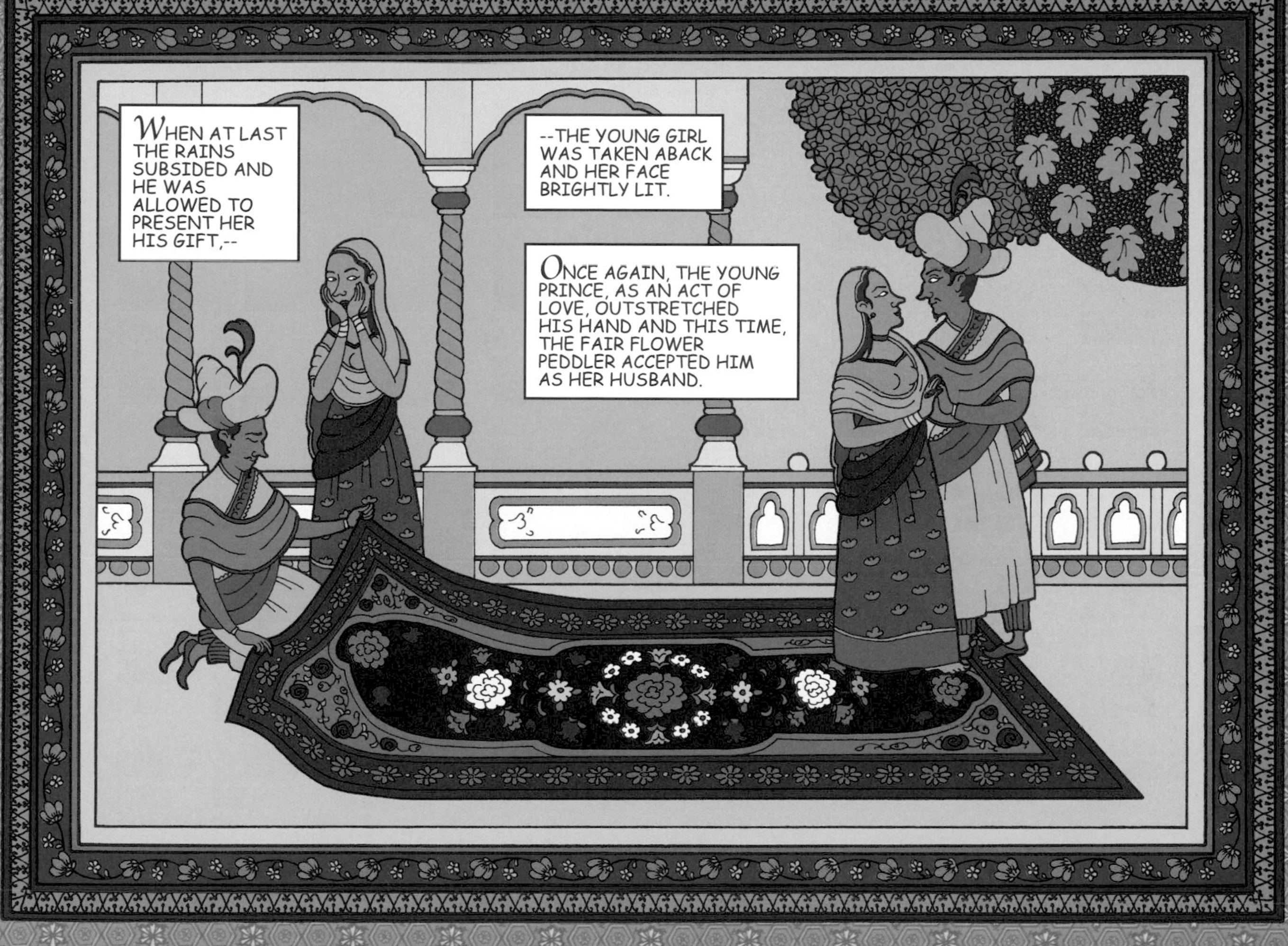
WHEN AT LAST THE RAINS SUBSIDED AND HE WAS ALLOWED TO PRESENT HER HIS GIFT,--
--THE YOUNG GIRL WAS TAKEN ABACK AND HER FACE BRIGHTLY LIT.
ONCE AGAIN, THE YOUNG PRINCE, AS AN ACT OF LOVE, OUTSTRETCHED HIS HAND AND THIS TIME, THE FAIR FLOWER PEDDLER ACCEPTED HIM AS HER HUSBAND.

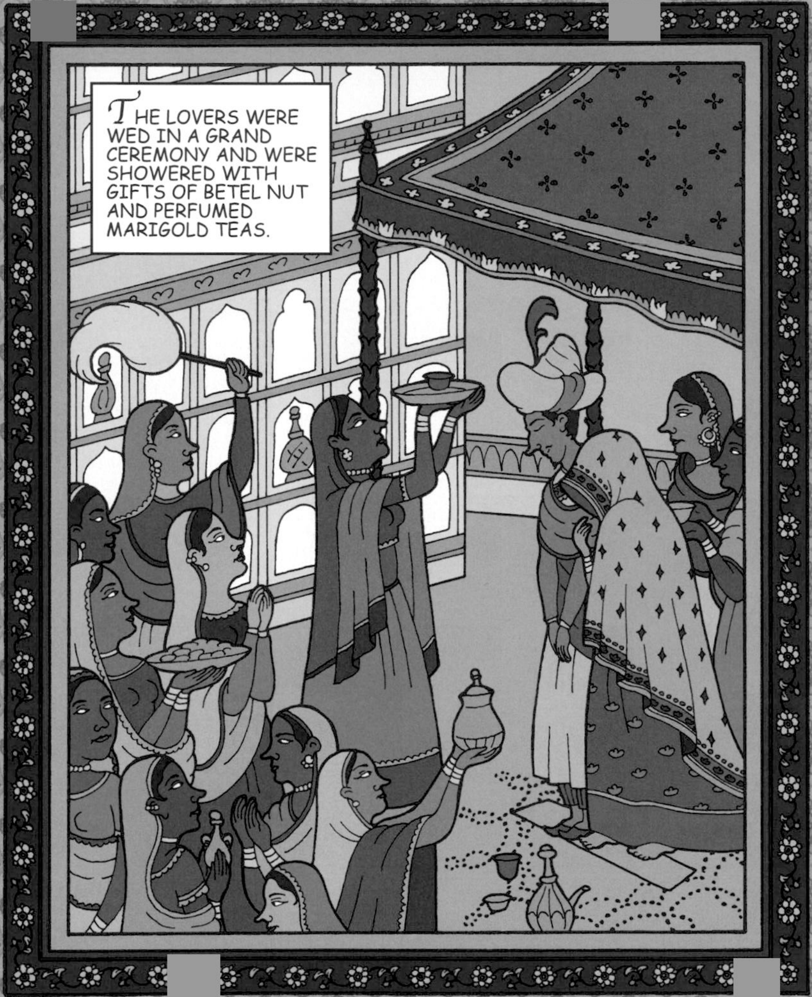
THE LOVERS WERE WED IN A GRAND CEREMONY AND WERE SHOWERED WITH GIFTS OF BETEL NUT AND PERFUMED MARIGOLD TEAS.

ON THE NIGHT THAT THEY WERE WED, THE YOUNG BRIDE CAME TO THE PRINCE AT THE FOOT OF HIS BED.

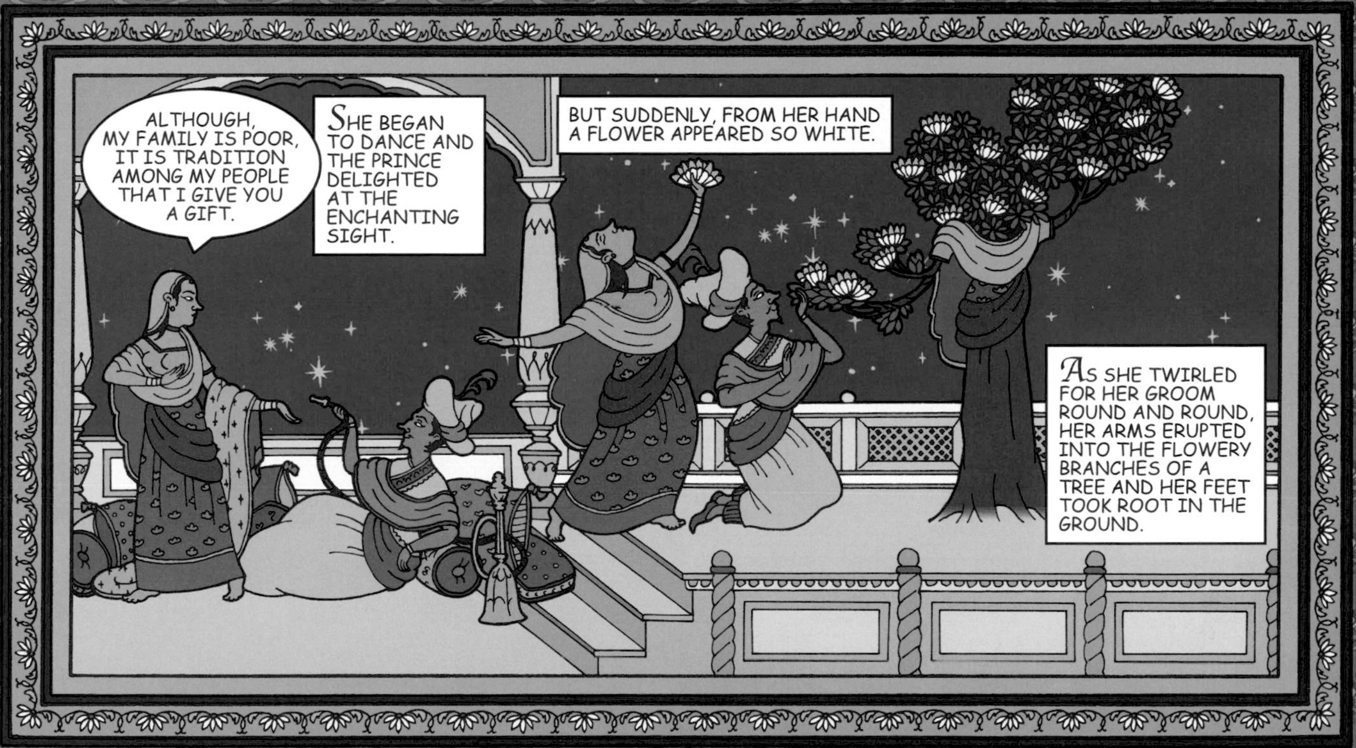
ALTHOUGH, MY FAMILY IS POOR, IT IS TRADITION AMONG MY PEOPLE THAT I GIVE YOU A GIFT.
SHE BEGAN TO DANCE AND THE PRINCE DELIGHTED AT THE ENCHANTING SIGHT.
BUT SUDDENLY, FROM HER HAND A FLOWER APPEARED SO WHITE.
AS SHE TWIRLED FOR HER GROOM ROUND AND ROUND, HER ARMS ERUPTED INTO THE FLOWERY BRANCHES OF A TREE AND HER FEET TOOK ROOT IN THE GROUND.

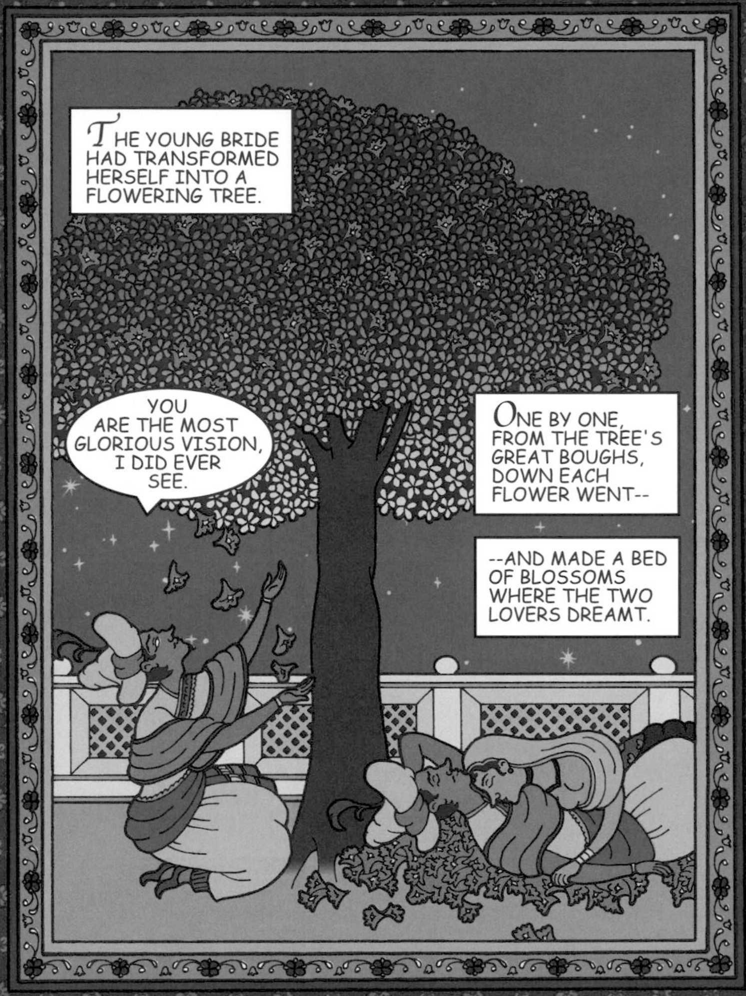
THE YOUNG BRIDE HAD TRANSFORMED HERSELF INTO A FLOWERING TREE.
YOU ARE THE MOST GLORIOUS VISION, I DID EVER SEE.
ONE BY ONE, FROM THE TREE'S GREAT BOUGHS, DOWN EACH FLOWER WENT--
--AND MADE A BED OF BLOSSOMS WHERE THE TWO LOVERS DREAMT.

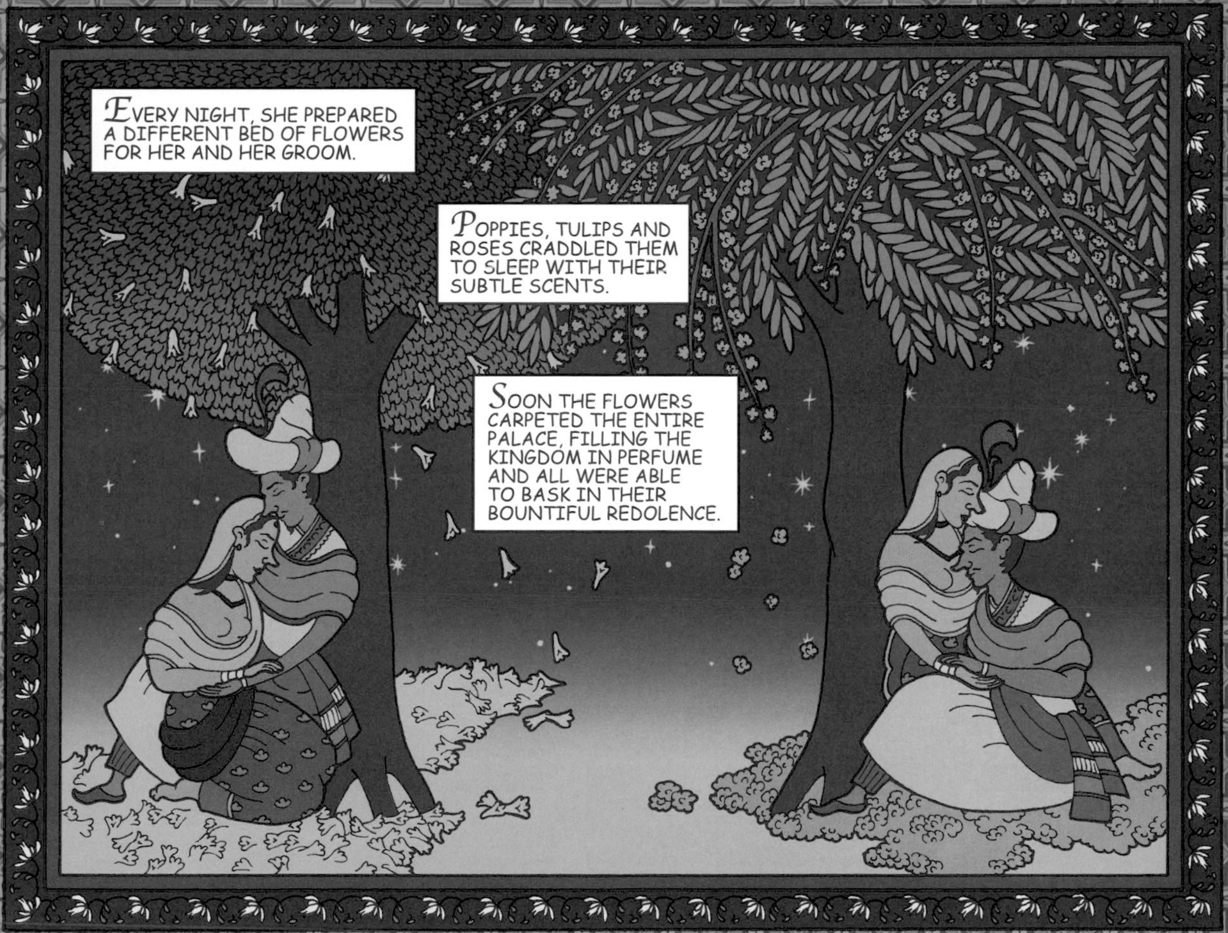
EVERY NIGHT, SHE PREPARED A DIFFERENT BED OF FLOWERS FOR HER AND HER GROOM.
POPPIES, TULIPS AND ROSES CRADDLED THEM TO SLEEP WITH THEIR SUBTLE SCENTS.
SOON THE FLOWERS CARPETED THE ENTIRE PALACE, FILLING THE KINGDOM IN PERFUME AND ALL WERE ABLE TO BASK IN THEIR BOUNTIFUL REDOLENCE.

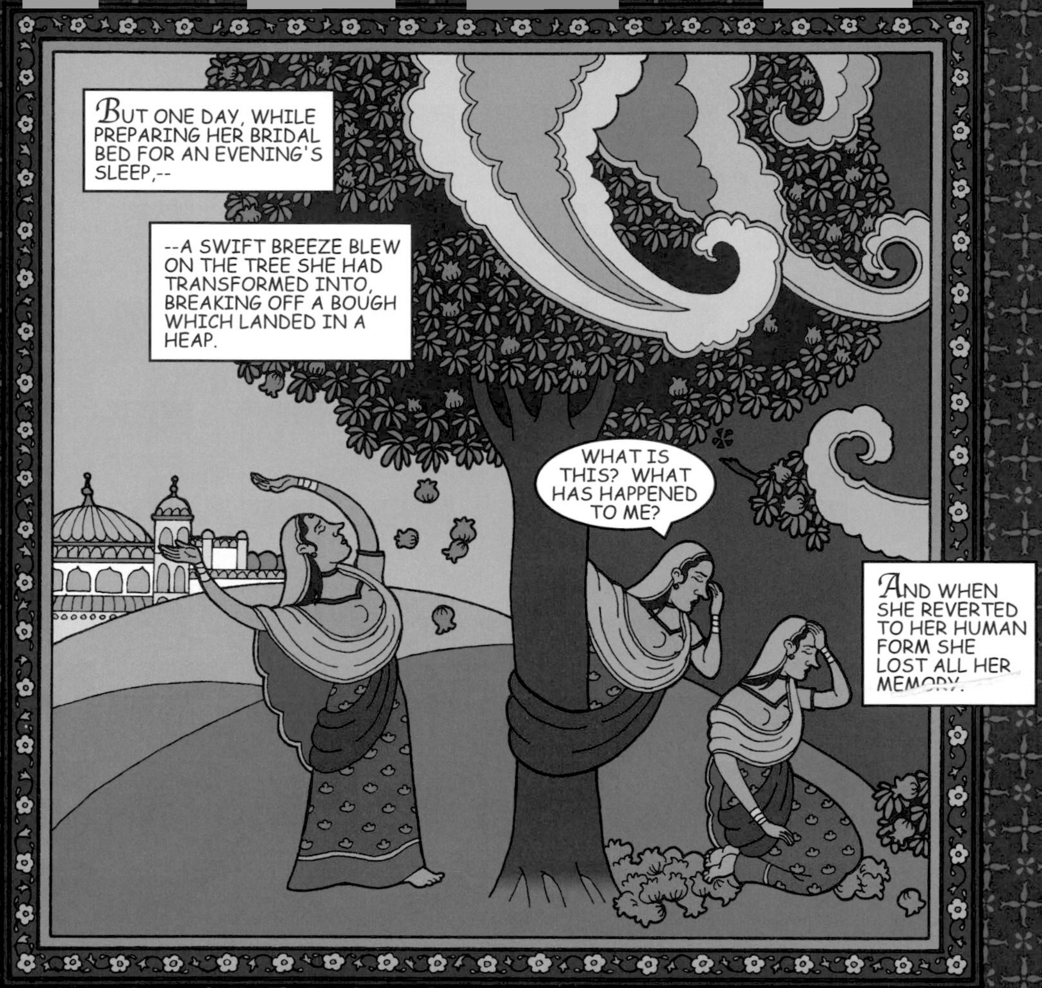
BUT ONE DAY, WHILE PREPARING HER BRIDAL BED FOR AN EVENING'S SLEEP,--
--A SWIFT BREEZE BLEW ON THE TREE SHE HAD TRANSFORMED INTO, BREAKING OFF A BOUGH WHICH LANDED IN A HEAP.
WHAT IS THIS? WHAT HAS HAPPENED TO ME?
AND WHEN SHE REVERTED TO HER HUMAN FORM SHE LOST ALL HER MEMORY.

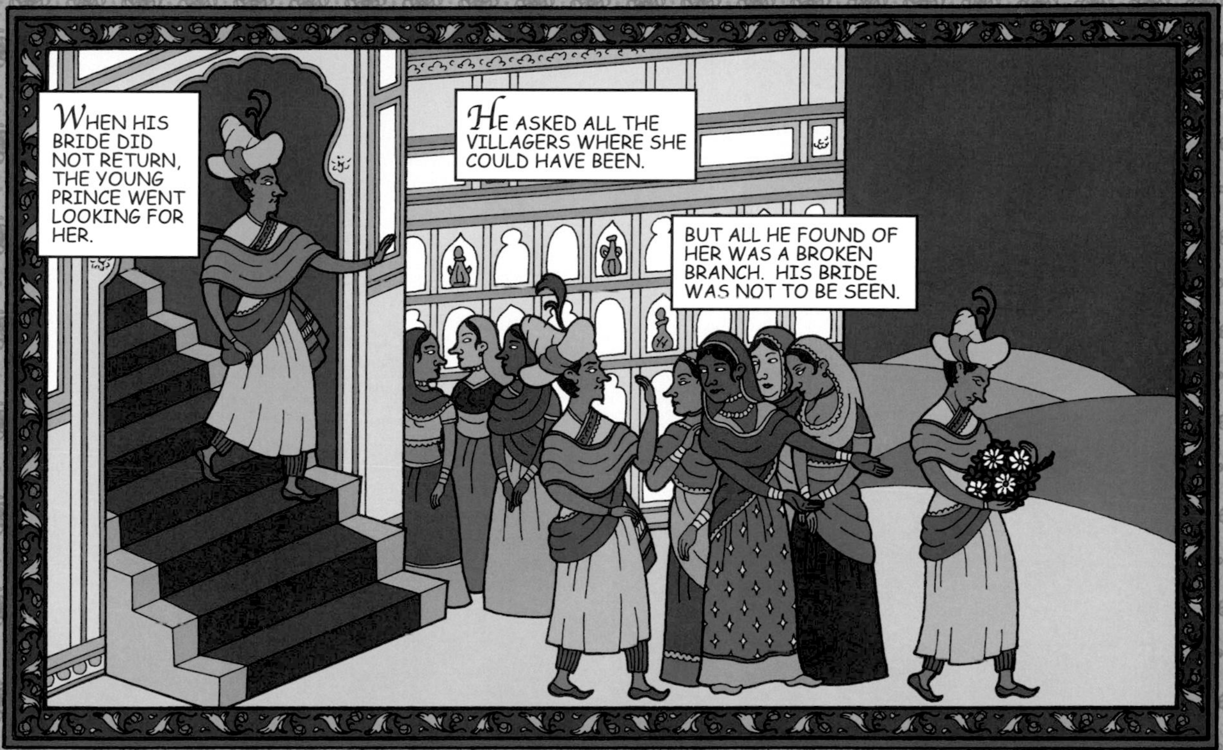
WHEN HIS BRIDE DID NOT RETURN, THE YOUNG PRINCE WENT LOOKING FOR HER.
HE ASKED ALL THE VILLAGERS WHERE SHE COULD HAVE BEEN.
BUT ALL HE FOUND OF HER WAS A BROKEN BRANCH. HIS BRIDE WAS NOT TO BE SEEN.

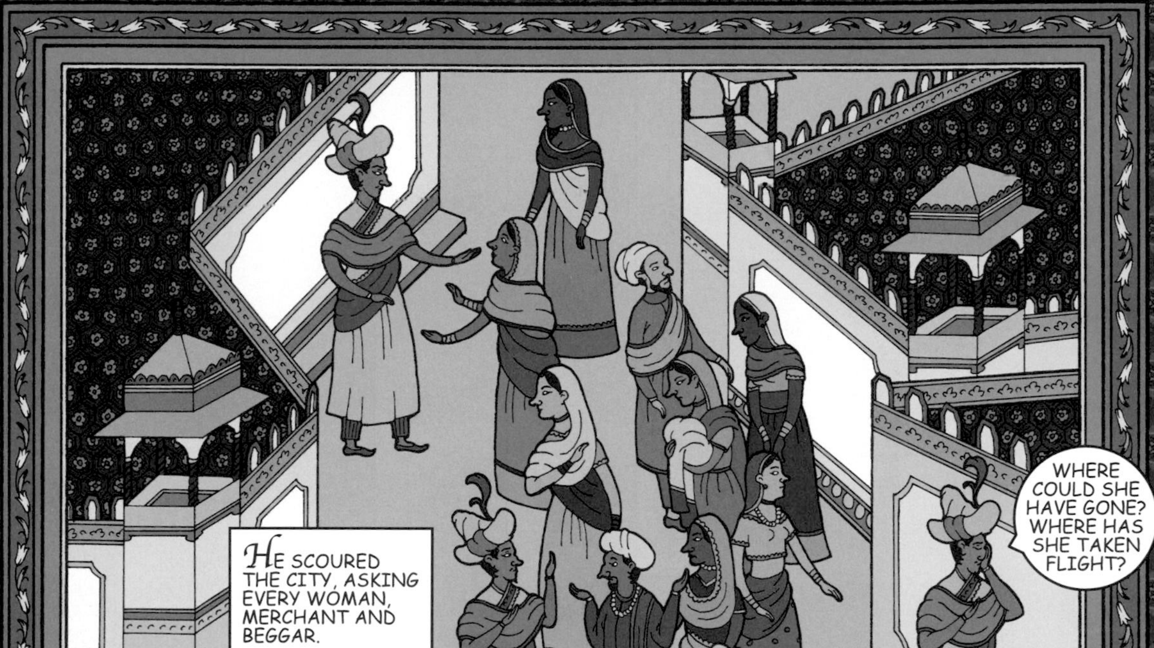
HE SCOURED THE CITY, ASKING EVERY WOMAN, MERCHANT AND BEGGAR.
BUT THEY COULD NOT HELP HIM. SHE WAS NOWHERE IN SIGHT.
WHERE COULD SHE HAVE GONE? WHERE HAS SHE TAKEN FLIGHT?

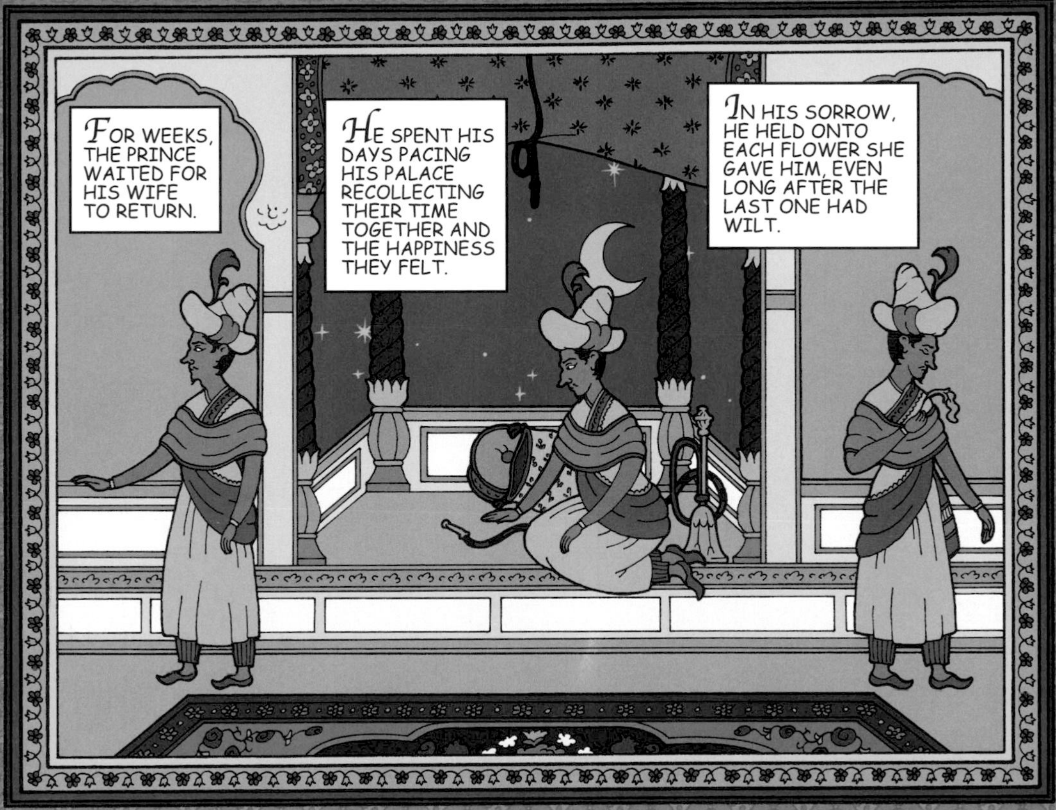
For weeks, the prince waited for his wife to return.
He spent his days pacing his palace recollecting their time together and the happiness they felt.
In his sorrow, he held onto each flower she gave him, even long after the last one had wilt.

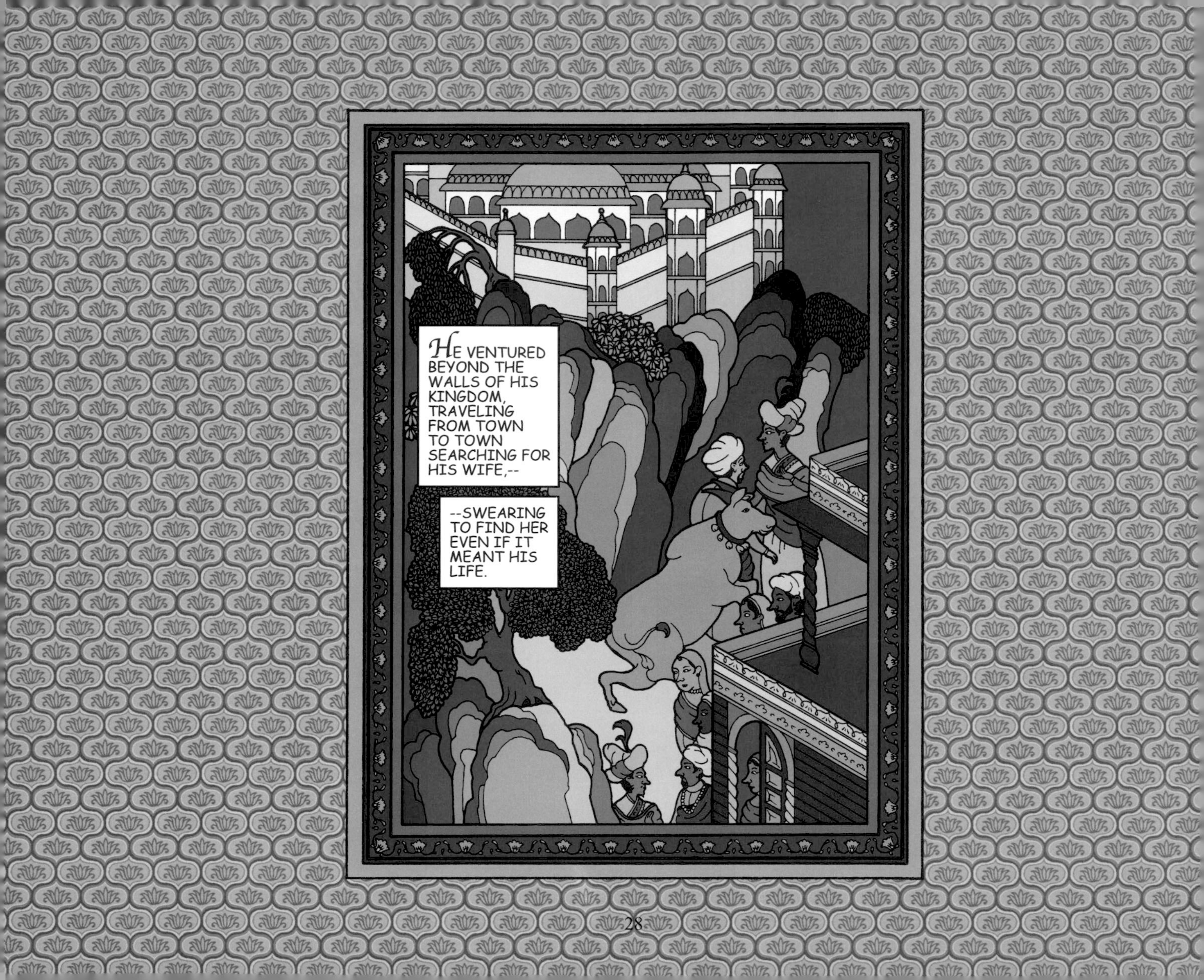
HE VENTURED BEYOND THE WALLS OF HIS KINGDOM, TRAVELING FROM TOWN TO TOWN SEARCHING FOR HIS WIFE,--
--SWEARING TO FIND HER EVEN IF IT MEANT HIS LIFE.

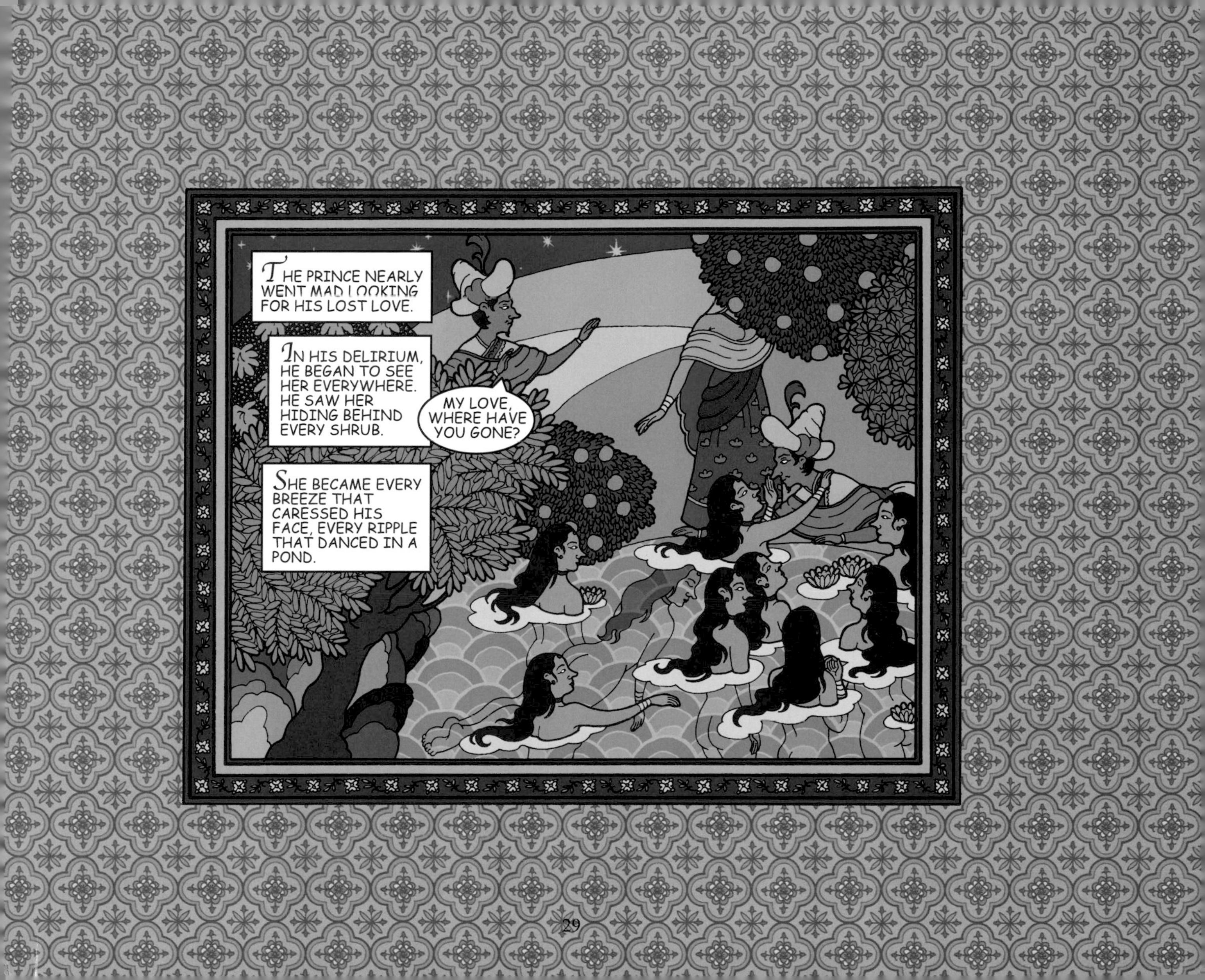
THE PRINCE NEARLY WENT MAD LOOKING FOR HIS LOST LOVE.
IN HIS DELIRIUM, HE BEGAN TO SEE HER EVERYWHERE. HE SAW HER HIDING BEHIND EVERY SHRUB.
MY LOVE, WHERE HAVE YOU GONE?
SHE BECAME EVERY BREEZE THAT CARESSED HIS FACE, EVERY RIPPLE THAT DANCED IN A POND.

AFTER YEARS OF WANDERING, LOST AND IN DESPAIR, THE PRINCE STILL HAD NOT FOUND HIS WIFE.
IT IS AS IF SHE HAD VANISHED INTO THIN AIR.
BUT STILL HE DID NOT STOP. HE SEARCHED EVERY TOWN AND EVERY TREE HE LAY UNDER.
UNTIL, FINALLY, HE WAS FOUND BY A YOUNG PRINCESS, HIS CLOTHING TATTERED AND HIS SPIRIT ASUNDER.

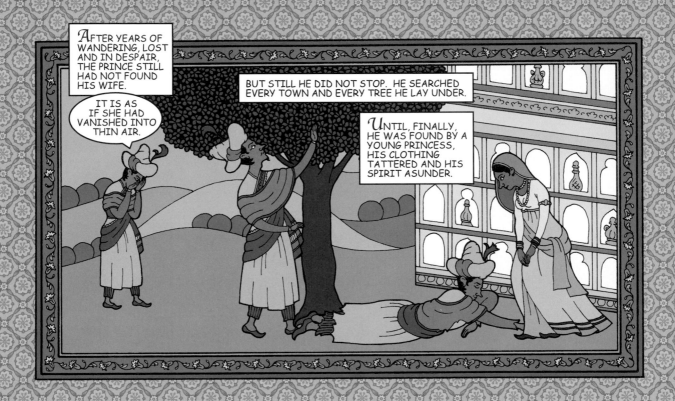

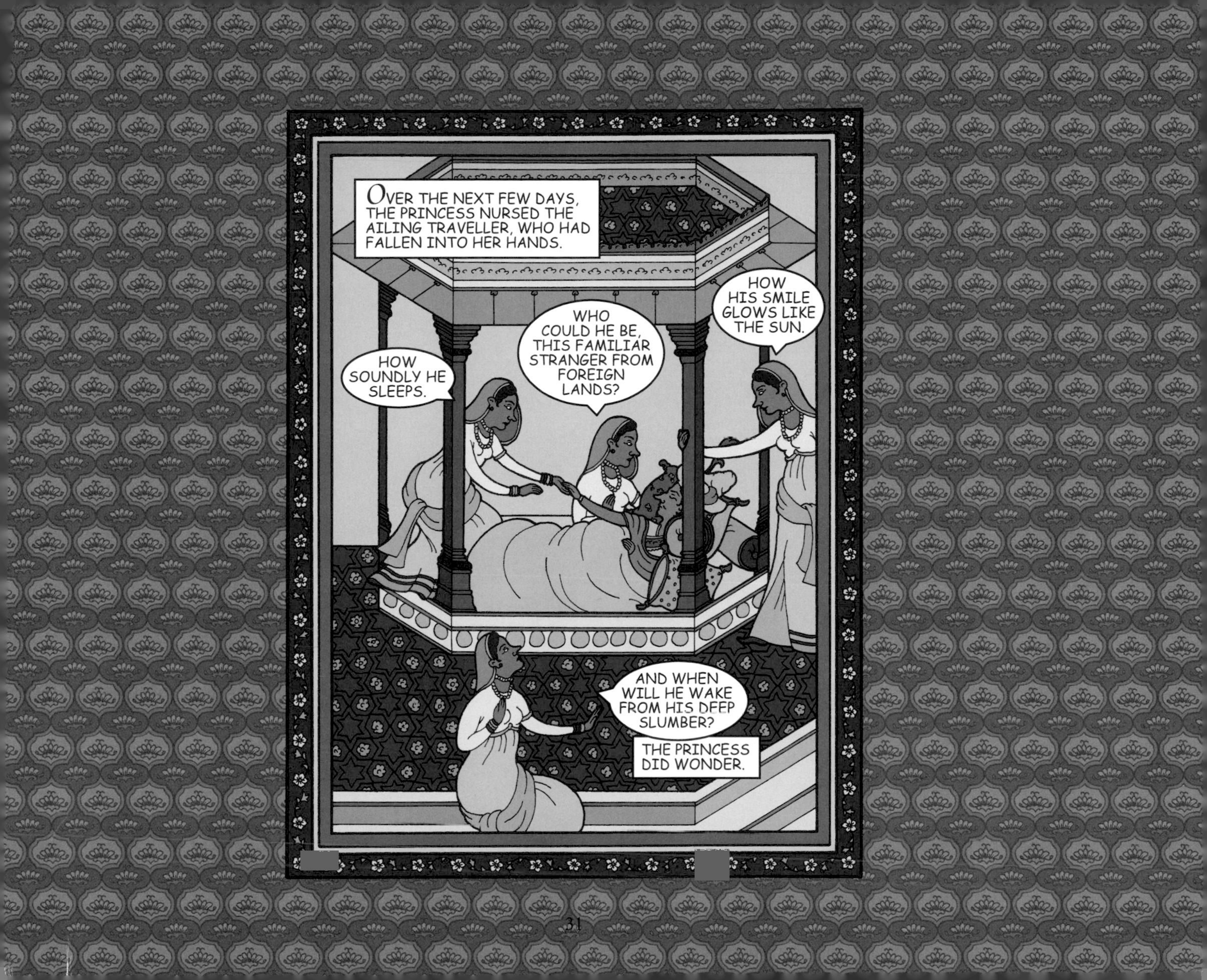
OVER THE NEXT FEW DAYS, THE PRINCESS NURSED THE AILING TRAVELLER, WHO HAD FALLEN INTO HER HANDS.
HOW SOUNDLY HE SLEEPS.
WHO COULD HE BE, THIS FAMILIAR STRANGER FROM FOREIGN LANDS?
HOW HIS SMILE GLOWS LIKE THE SUN.
AND WHEN WILL HE WAKE FROM HIS DEEP SLUMBER?
THE PRINCESS DID WONDER.

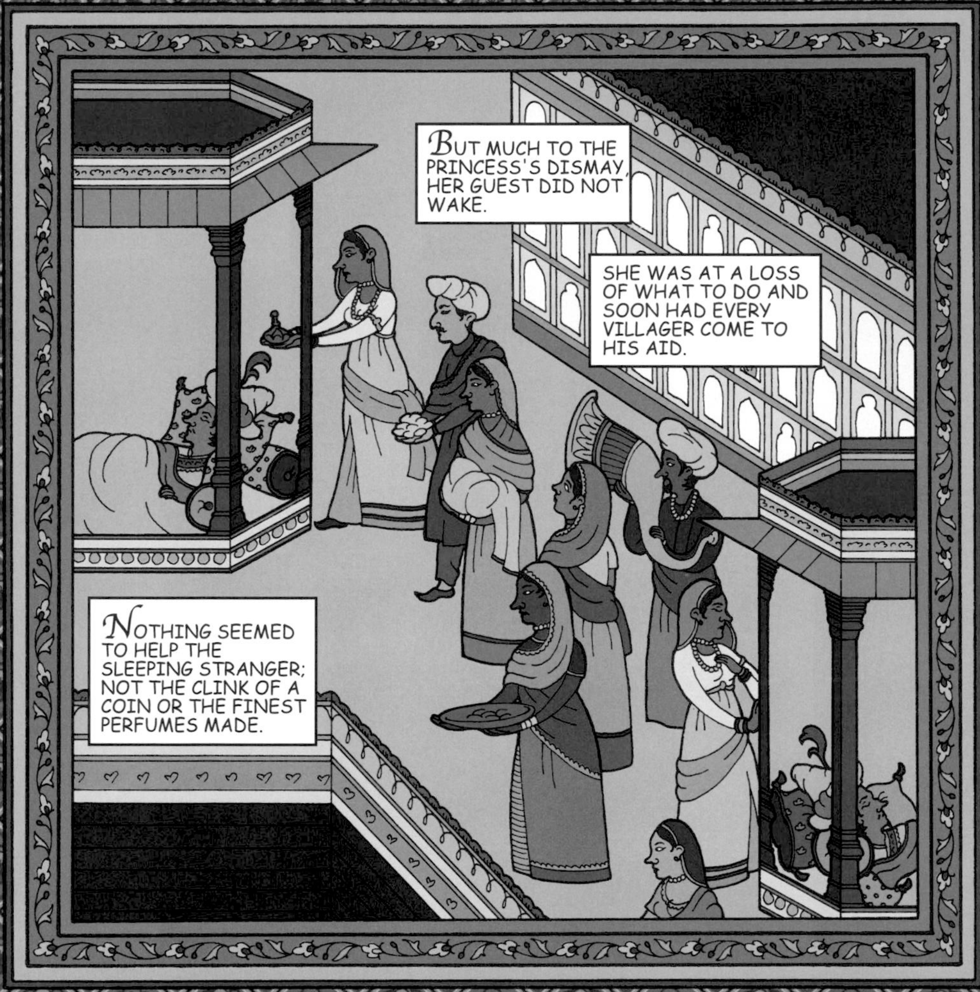
BUT MUCH TO THE PRINCESS'S DISMAY, HER GUEST DID NOT WAKE.
SHE WAS AT A LOSS OF WHAT TO DO AND SOON HAD EVERY VILLAGER COME TO HIS AID.
NOTHING SEEMED TO HELP THE SLEEPING STRANGER; NOT THE CLINK OF A COIN OR THE FINEST PERFUMES MADE.

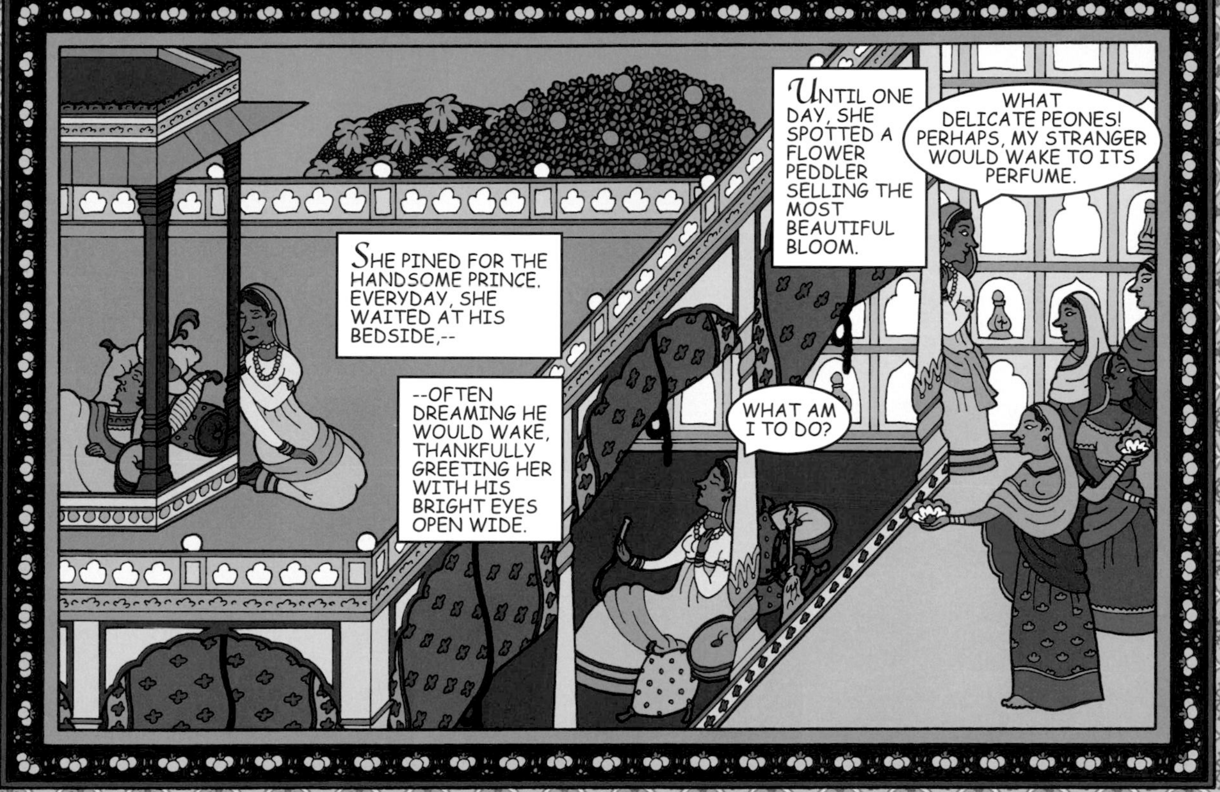
SHE PINED FOR THE HANDSOME PRINCE. EVERYDAY, SHE WAITED AT HIS BEDSIDE,--
--OFTEN DREAMING HE WOULD WAKE, THANKFULLY GREETING HER WITH HIS BRIGHT EYES OPEN WIDE.
UNTIL ONE DAY, SHE SPOTTED A FLOWER PEDDLER SELLING THE MOST BEAUTIFUL BLOOM.
WHAT AM I TO DO?
WHAT DELICATE PEONES! PERHAPS, MY STRANGER WOULD WAKE TO ITS PERFUME.

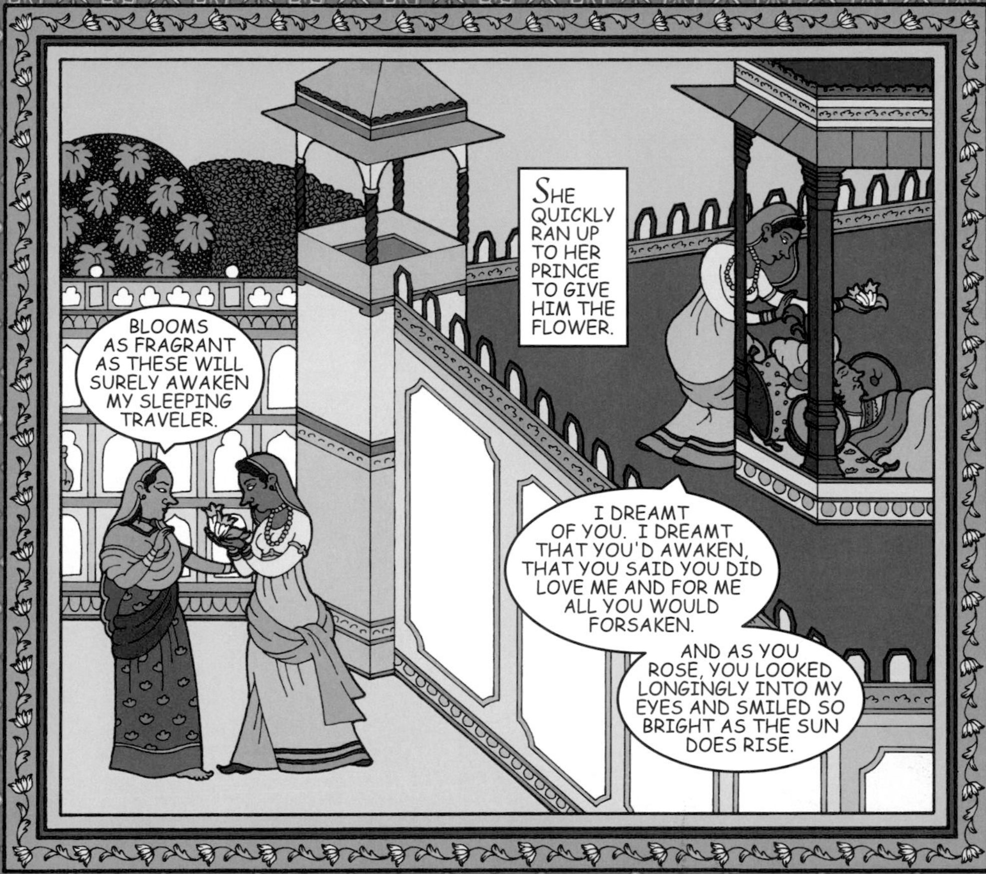
BLOOMS AS FRAGRANT AS THESE WILL SURELY AWAKEN MY SLEEPING TRAVELER.
SHE QUICKLY RAN UP TO HER PRINCE TO GIVE HIM THE FLOWER.
I DREAMT OF YOU. I DREAMT THAT YOU'D AWAKEN, THAT YOU SAID YOU DID LOVE ME AND FOR ME ALL YOU WOULD FORSAKEN.
AND AS YOU ROSE, YOU LOOKED LONGINGLY INTO MY EYES AND SMILED SO BRIGHT AS THE SUN DOES RISE.

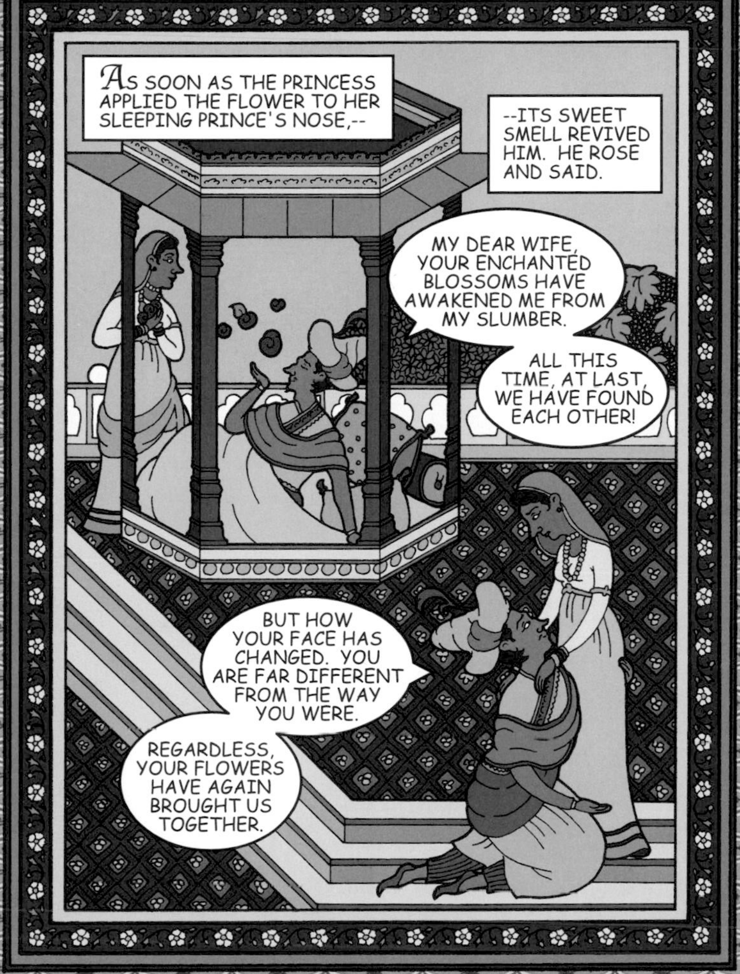
As soon as the princess applied the flower to her sleeping prince's nose,--
--ITS SWEET SMELL REVIVED HIM. HE ROSE AND SAID.
MY DEAR WIFE, YOUR ENCHANTED BLOSSOMS HAVE AWAKENED ME FROM MY SLUMBER.
ALL THIS TIME, AT LAST, WE HAVE FOUND EACH OTHER!
BUT HOW YOUR FACE HAS CHANGED. YOU ARE FAR DIFFERENT FROM THE WAY YOU WERE.
REGARDLESS, YOUR FLOWERS HAVE AGAIN BROUGHT US TOGETHER.

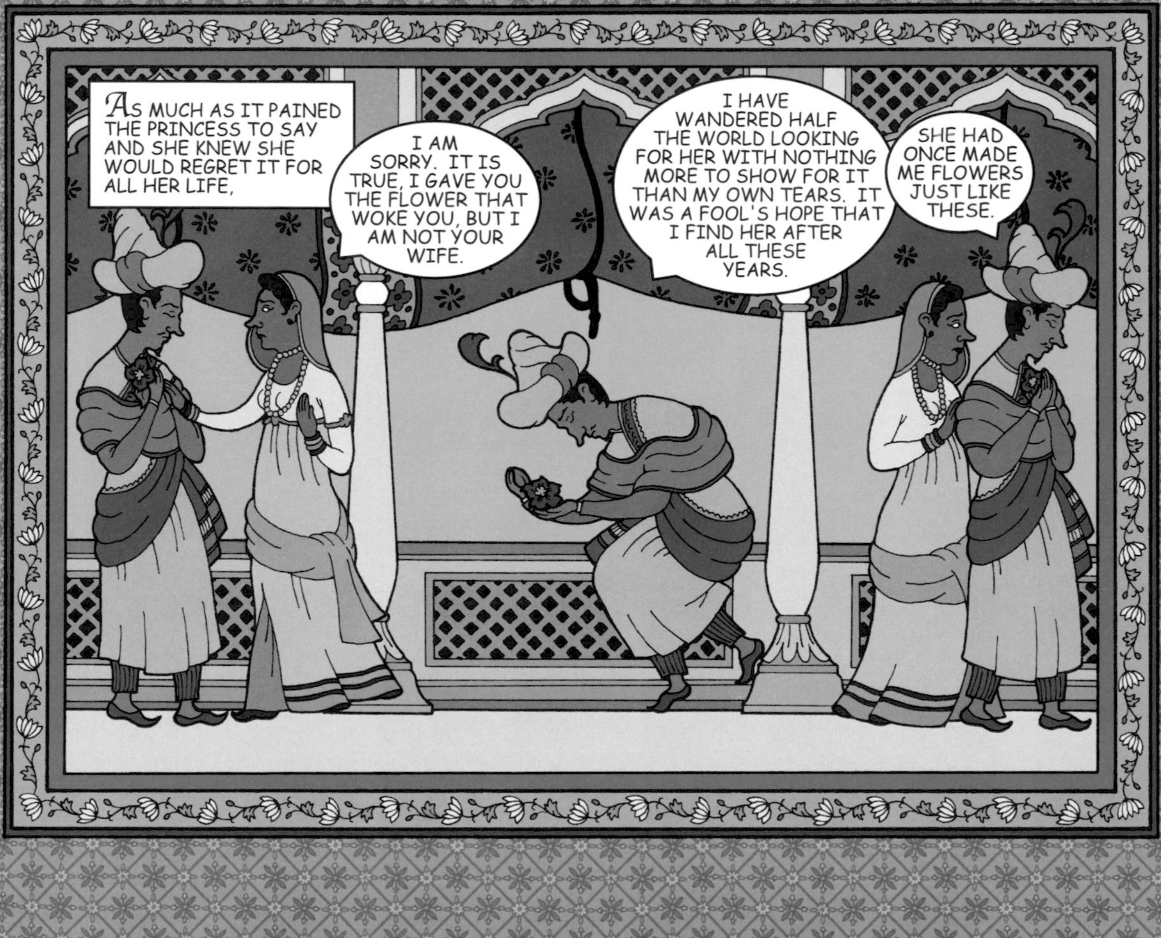
AS MUCH AS IT PAINED THE PRINCESS TO SAY AND SHE KNEW SHE WOULD REGRET IT FOR ALL HER LIFE,
I AM SORRY. IT IS TRUE, I GAVE YOU THE FLOWER THAT WOKE YOU, BUT I AM NOT YOUR WIFE.
I HAVE WANDERED HALF THE WORLD LOOKING FOR HER WITH NOTHING MORE TO SHOW FOR IT THAN MY OWN TEARS. IT WAS A FOOL'S HOPE THAT I FIND HER AFTER ALL THESE YEARS.
SHE HAD ONCE MADE ME FLOWERS JUST LIKE THESE.

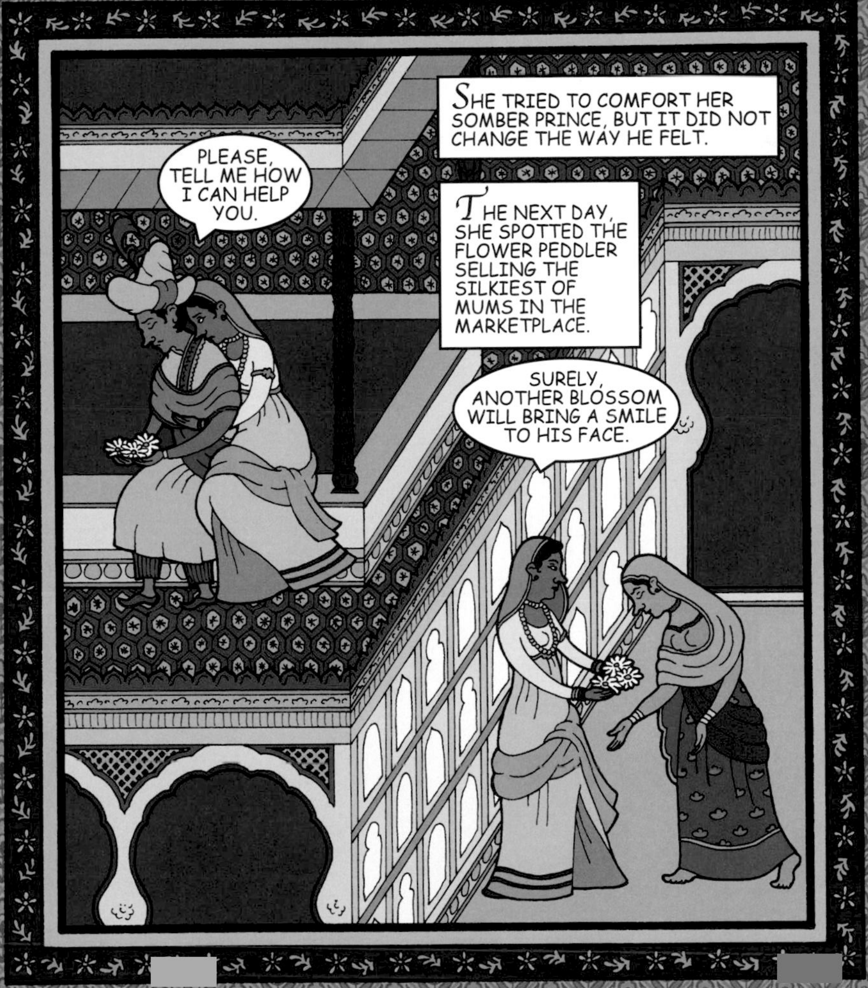
PLEASE, TELL ME HOW I CAN HELP YOU.
SHE TRIED TO COMFORT HER SOMBER PRINCE, BUT IT DID NOT CHANGE THE WAY HE FELT.
THE NEXT DAY, SHE SPOTTED THE FLOWER PEDDLER SELLING THE SILKIEST OF MUMS IN THE MARKETPLACE.
SURELY, ANOTHER BLOSSOM WILL BRING A SMILE TO HIS FACE.

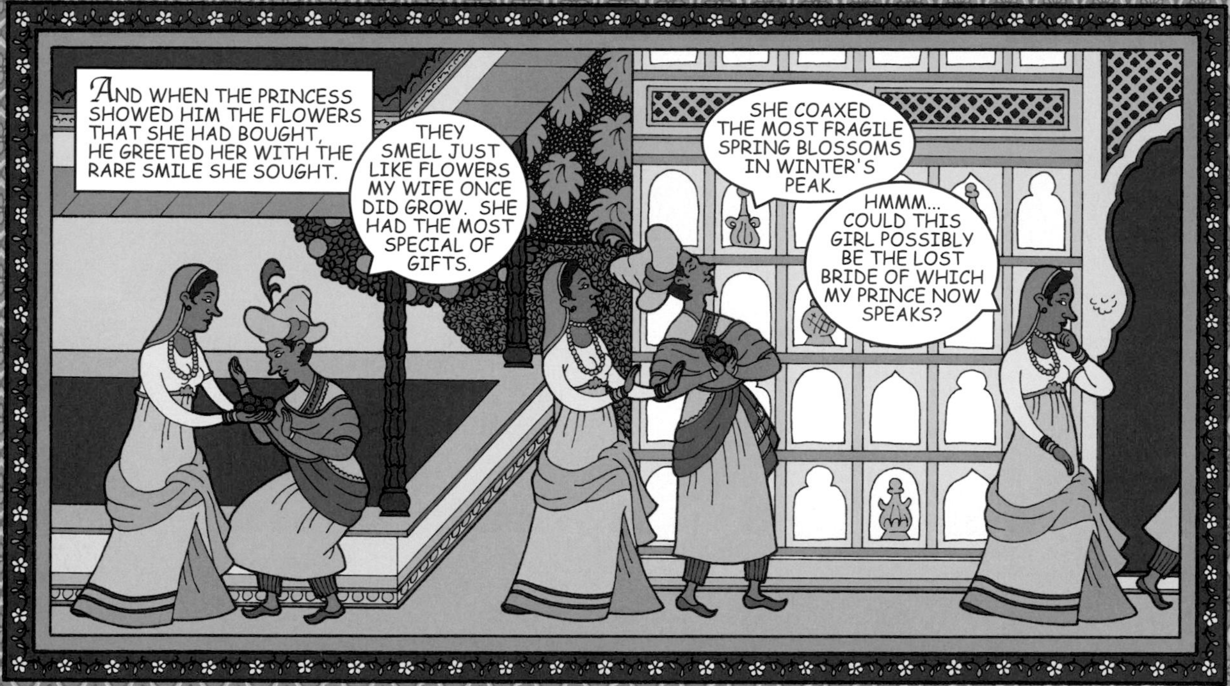
AND WHEN THE PRINCESS SHOWED HIM THE FLOWERS THAT SHE HAD BOUGHT, HE GREETED HER WITH THE RARE SMILE SHE SOUGHT.
THEY SMELL JUST LIKE FLOWERS MY WIFE ONCE DID GROW. SHE HAD THE MOST SPECIAL OF GIFTS.
SHE COAXED THE MOST FRAGILE SPRING BLOSSOMS IN WINTER'S PEAK.
HMMM... COULD THIS GIRL POSSIBLY BE THE LOST BRIDE OF WHICH MY PRINCE NOW SPEAKS?

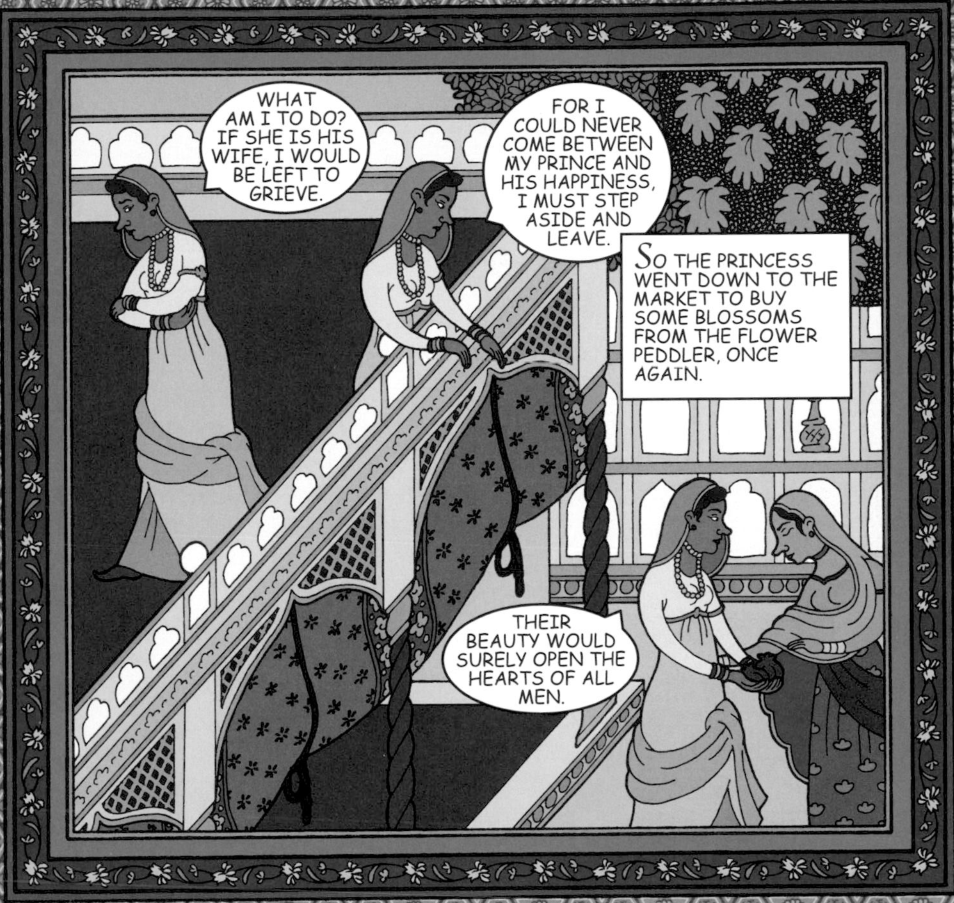
WHAT AM I TO DO? IF SHE IS HIS WIFE, I WOULD BE LEFT TO GRIEVE.
FOR I COULD NEVER COME BETWEEN MY PRINCE AND HIS HAPPINESS, I MUST STEP ASIDE AND LEAVE.
SO THE PRINCESS WENT DOWN TO THE MARKET TO BUY SOME BLOSSOMS FROM THE FLOWER PEDDLER, ONCE AGAIN.
THEIR BEAUTY WOULD SURELY OPEN THE HEARTS OF ALL MEN.

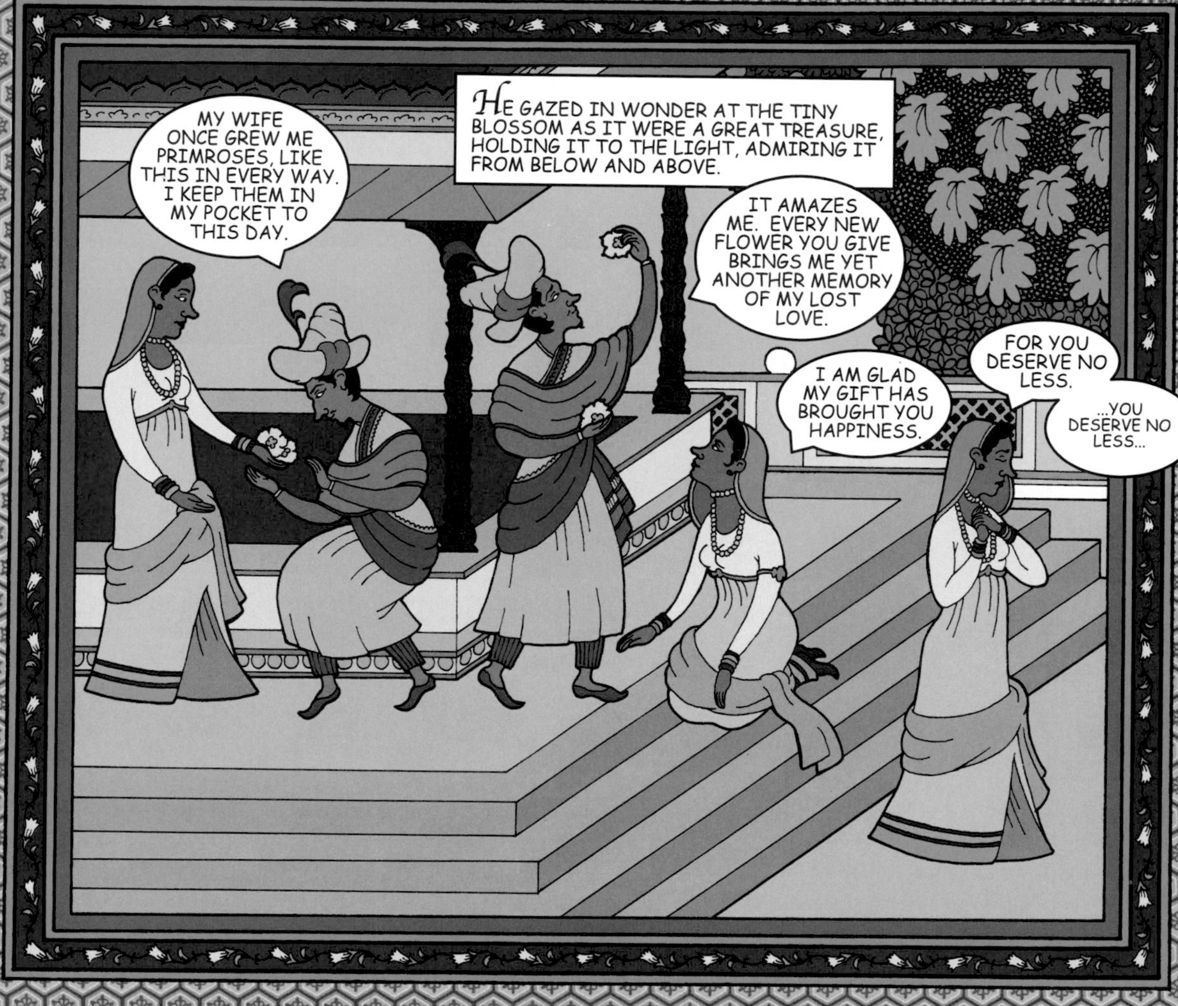
HE GAZED IN WONDER AT THE TINY BLOSSOM AS IT WERE A GREAT TREASURE, HOLDING IT TO THE LIGHT, ADMIRING IT FROM BELOW AND ABOVE.
MY WIFE ONCE GREW ME PRIMROSES, LIKE THIS IN EVERY WAY. I KEEP THEM IN MY POCKET TO THIS DAY.
IT AMAZES ME. EVERY NEW FLOWER YOU GIVE BRINGS ME YET ANOTHER MEMORY OF MY LOST LOVE.
I AM GLAD MY GIFT HAS BROUGHT YOU HAPPINESS.
FOR YOU DESERVE NO LESS.
...YOU DESERVE NO LESS...

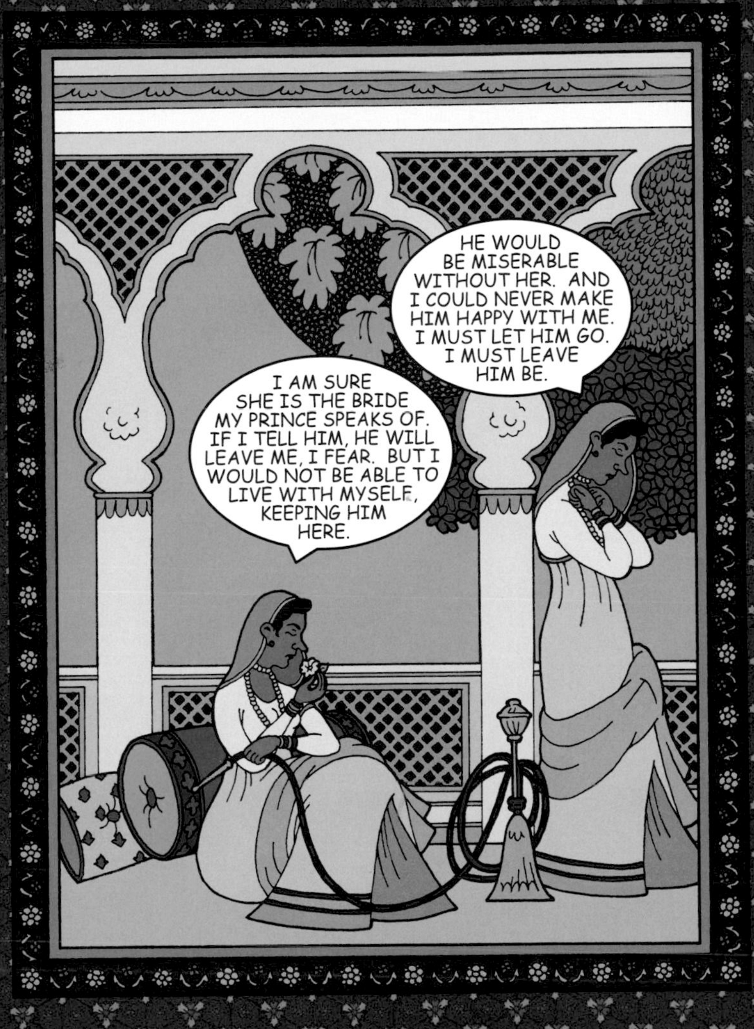
I AM SURE SHE IS THE BRIDE MY PRINCE SPEAKS OF. IF I TELL HIM, HE WILL LEAVE ME, I FEAR. BUT I WOULD NOT BE ABLE TO LIVE WITH MYSELF, KEEPING HIM HERE.
HE WOULD BE MISERABLE WITHOUT HER. AND I COULD NEVER MAKE HIM HAPPY WITH ME. I MUST LET HIM GO. I MUST LEAVE HIM BE.

HEAVY-HEARTED, SHE SENT THE PRINCE OFF TO THE LOCAL MARKET, FEIGNING ILLNESS.

WOULD YOU GO FETCH THIS MORNING'S FLOWERS?
WHY OF COURSE, MY FAIR PRINCESS.
BUT WHEN THE PRINCE ARRIVED AT THE MARKET, HE WAS STRUCK WITH A VISION. HE COULDN'T BELIEVE WHAT HE WAS SEEING.
HE BLINKED HIS EYES IN DISBELIEF AND FROZE IN A STARE.
COULD THIS BE? AM I DREAMING?

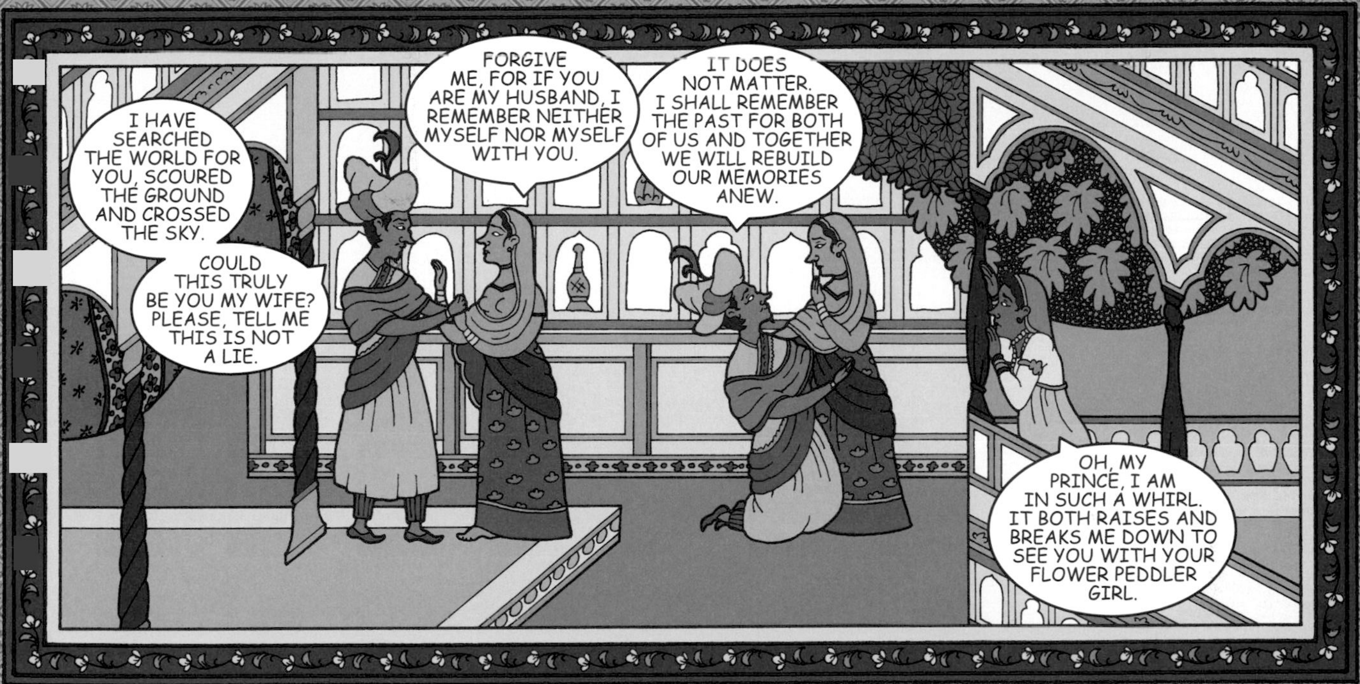
I HAVE SEARCHED THE WORLD FOR YOU, SCOURED THE GROUND AND CROSSED THE SKY.
COULD THIS TRULY BE YOU MY WIFE? PLEASE, TELL ME THIS IS NOT A LIE.
FORGIVE ME, FOR IF YOU ARE MY HUSBAND, I REMEMBER NEITHER MYSELF NOR MYSELF WITH YOU.
IT DOES NOT MATTER. I SHALL REMEMBER THE PAST FOR BOTH OF US AND TOGETHER WE WILL REBUILD OUR MEMORIES ANEW.
OH, MY PRINCE, I AM IN SUCH A WHIRL. IT BOTH RAISES AND BREAKS ME DOWN TO SEE YOU WITH YOUR FLOWER PEDDLER GIRL.

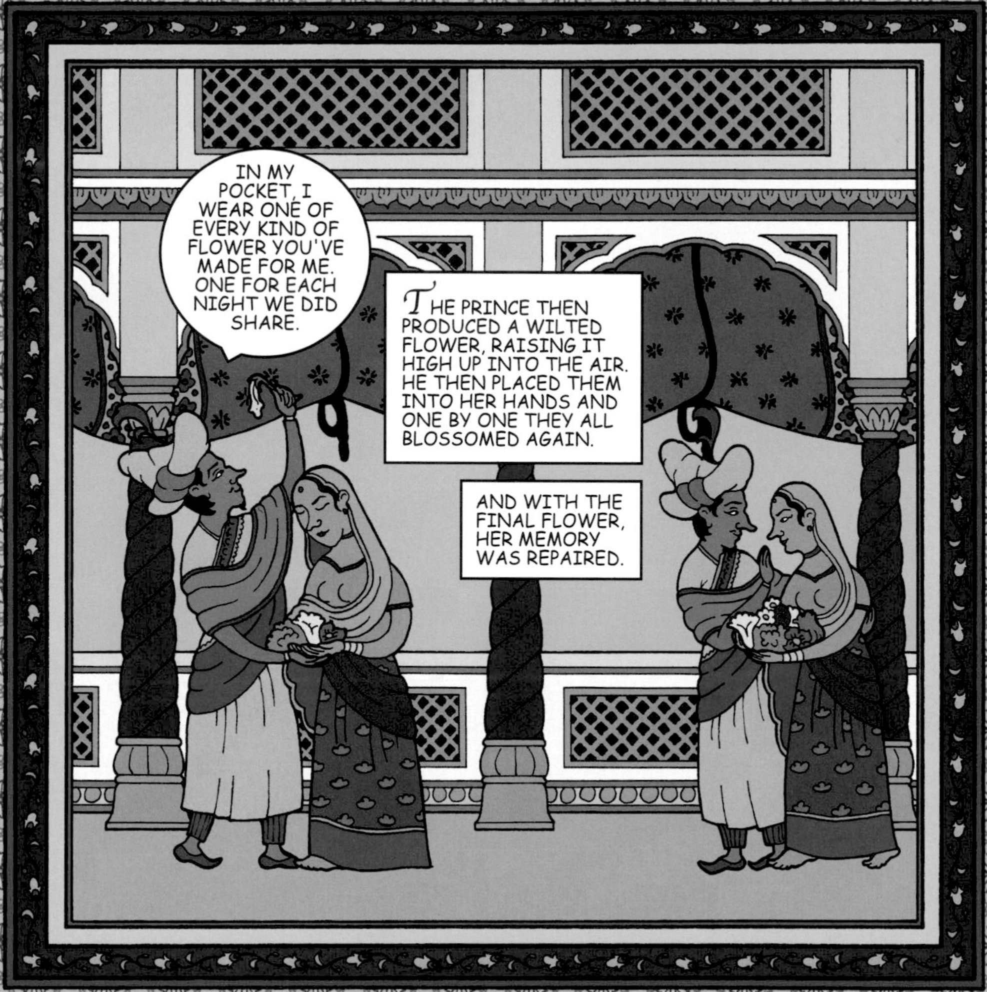
IN MY POCKET, I WEAR ONE OF EVERY KIND OF FLOWER YOU'VE MADE FOR ME. ONE FOR EACH NIGHT WE DID SHARE.
THE PRINCE THEN PRODUCED A WILTED FLOWER, RAISING IT HIGH UP INTO THE AIR. HE THEN PLACED THEM INTO HER HANDS AND ONE BY ONE THEY ALL BLOSSOMED AGAIN.
AND WITH THE FINAL FLOWER, HER MEMORY WAS REPAIRED.

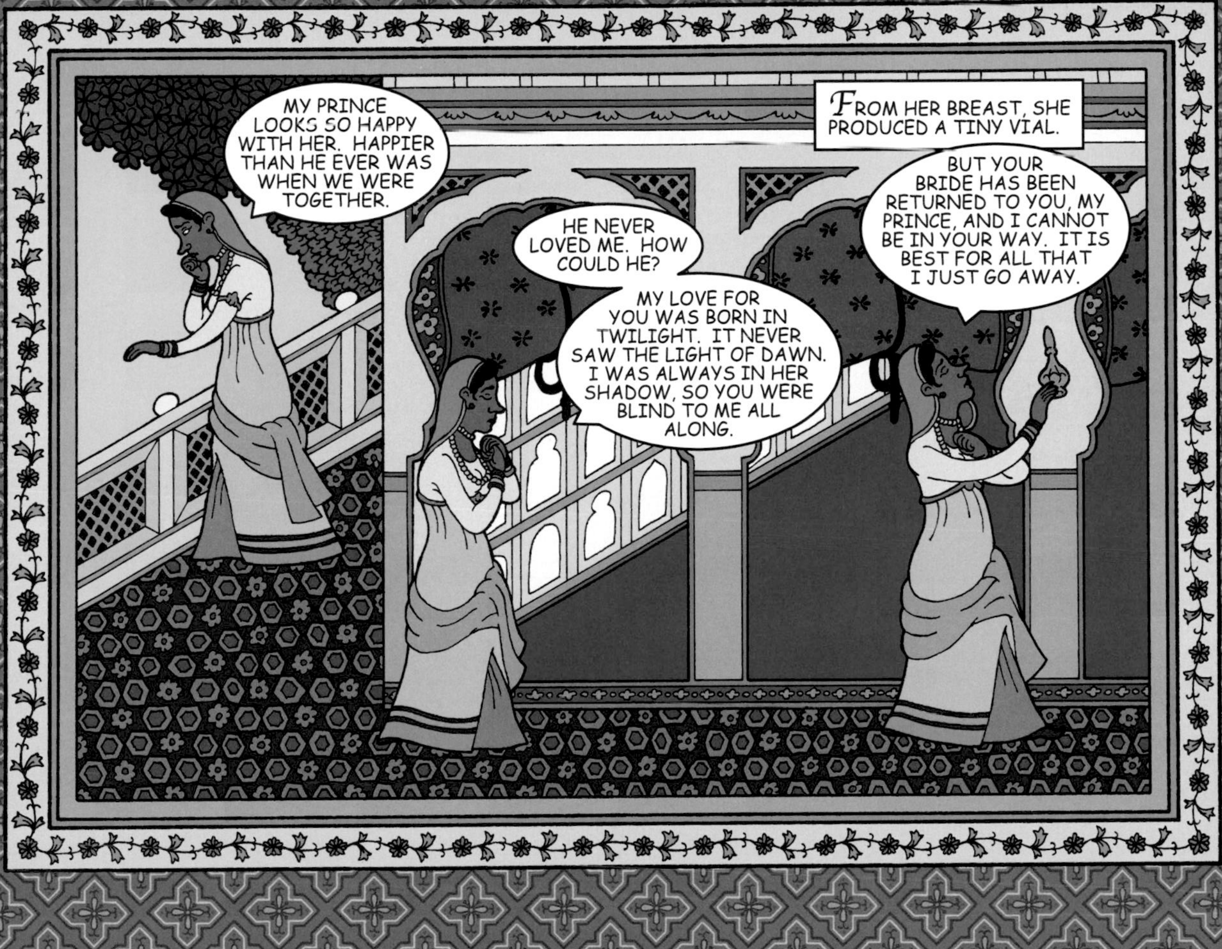
MY PRINCE LOOKS SO HAPPY WITH HER. HAPPIER THAN HE EVER WAS WHEN WE WERE TOGETHER.
HE NEVER LOVED ME. HOW COULD HE?
MY LOVE FOR YOU WAS BORN IN TWILIGHT. IT NEVER SAW THE LIGHT OF DAWN. I WAS ALWAYS IN HER SHADOW, SO YOU WERE BLIND TO ME ALL ALONG.
FROM HER BREAST, SHE PRODUCED A TINY VIAL.
BUT YOUR BRIDE HAS BEEN RETURNED TO YOU, MY PRINCE, AND I CANNOT BE IN YOUR WAY. IT IS BEST FOR ALL THAT I JUST GO AWAY.

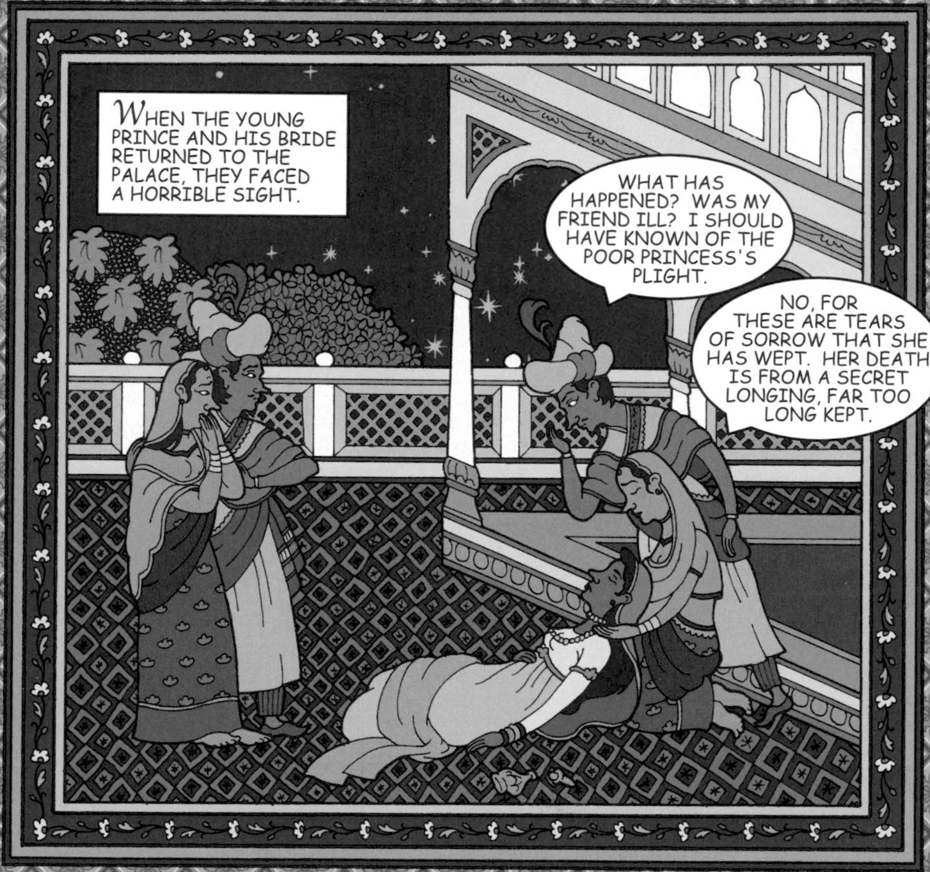
WHEN THE YOUNG PRINCE AND HIS BRIDE RETURNED TO THE PALACE, THEY FACED A HORRIBLE SIGHT.
WHAT HAS HAPPENED? WAS MY FRIEND ILL? I SHOULD HAVE KNOWN OF THE POOR PRINCESS'S PLIGHT.
NO, FOR THESE ARE TEARS OF SORROW THAT SHE HAS WEPT. HER DEATH IS FROM A SECRET LONGING, FAR TOO LONG KEPT.

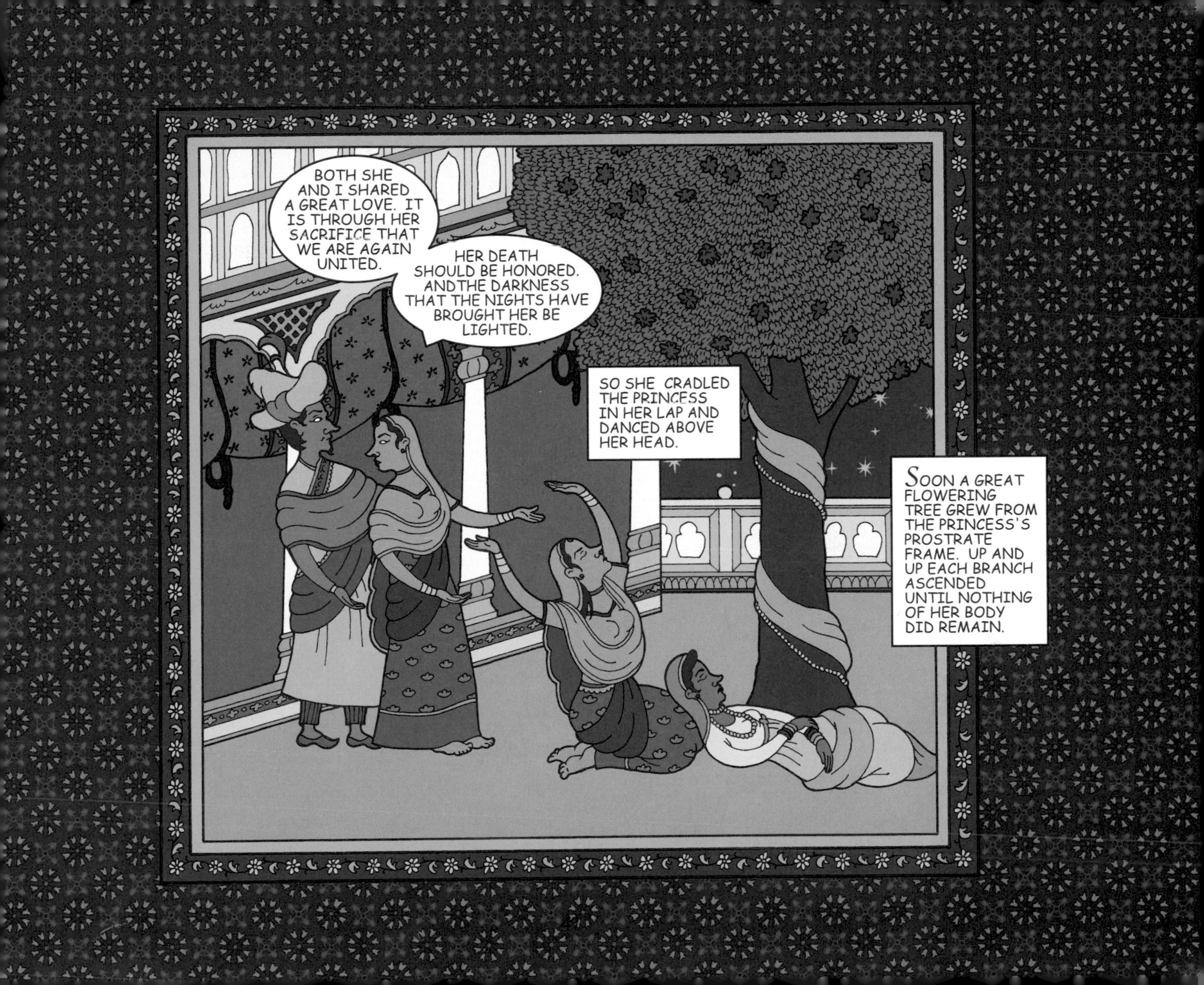
BOTH SHE AND I SHARED A GREAT LOVE. IT IS THROUGH HER SACRIFICE THAT WE ARE AGAIN UNITED.
HER DEATH SHOULD BE HONORED. AND THE DARKNESS THAT THE NIGHTS HAVE BROUGHT HER BE LIGHTED.
SO SHE CRADLED THE PRINCESS IN HER LAP AND DANCED ABOVE HER HEAD.
SOON A GREAT FLOWERING TREE GREW FROM THE PRINCESS'S PROSTRATE FRAME. UP AND UP EACH BRANCH ASCENDED UNTIL NOTHING OF HER BODY DID REMAIN.

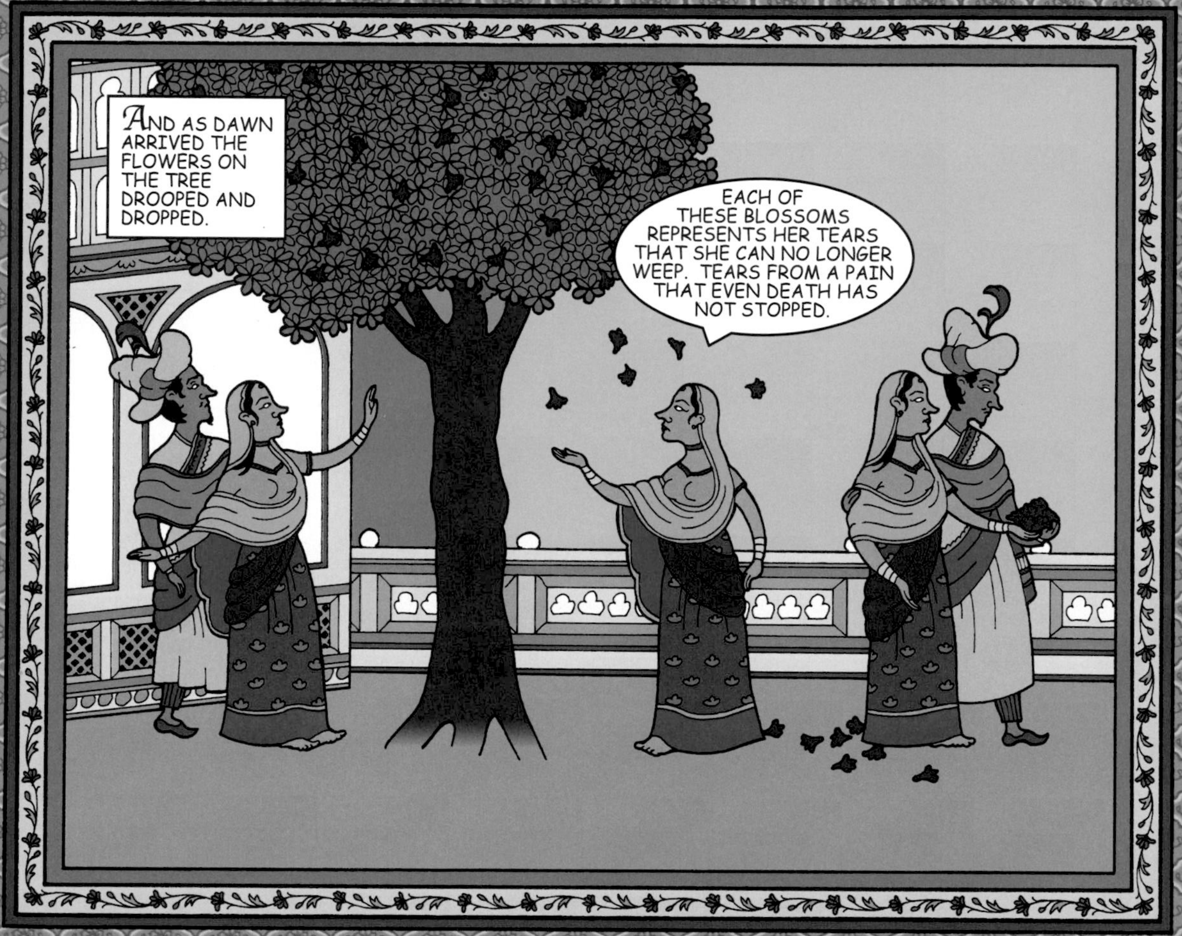
AND AS DAWN ARRIVED THE FLOWERS ON THE TREE DROOPED AND DROPPED.
EACH OF THESE BLOSSOMS REPRESENTS HER TEARS THAT SHE CAN NO LONGER WEEP. TEARS FROM A PAIN THAT EVEN DEATH HAS NOT STOPPED.